Grammatix

Grammar in context

A creative and inspiring guide to the theory and use of grammar, for teachers, parents and pupils

Sarah North

ISEB

Independent Schools
Examinations Board

First published 2020

by John Catt Educational Ltd,
15 Riduna Park, Station Road,
Melton, Woodbridge IP12 1QT

Tel: +44 (0) 1394 389850
Email: enquiries@johncatt.com
Website: www.johncatt.com

ISBN: 978 1 913622 05 3

Set and designed by John Catt Educational Ltd

Pigeons **by Richard Kell (p35)**: Every effort has
been made to trace the copyright holders and
obtain permission to reproduce this material.

Child on Top of a Greenhouse **by Theodore
Roethke (p39)**: Copyright © 1946 by Editorial
Publications, Inc. © 1699, renewed 1994 by
Beatrice Lushington from *Collected Poems*
by Theodore Roethke, Faber & Faber Ltd,
1968, pp.43. Reproduced by permission of the
publisher.

Warning **by Jenny Joseph (p44)**: Copyright
© Jenny Joseph, *Selected Poems*, Bloodaxe,
1992. Reproduced with permission of Johnson
& Alcock Ltd.

The Railings **by Roger McGough (p57)**:
Copyright © Roger McGough, *Collected
Poems*, Penguin UK, 2004. Reproduced by
permission of the publisher.

TESTIMONIALS

Sarah is an outstanding teacher of English and has inspired the many children she has taught over the years. Not only is she an enormously creative teacher but she has also managed to combine this with a talent for covering the many aspects of grammar that have too often been neglected, or not taught well. Her pupils have therefore had the best of both worlds and I am so pleased she is now sharing her resources and years of experience. I commend this excellent book to every English teacher who values the importance of taking a comprehensive and high-class approach to the teaching of grammar.

Andrew Nott, former headmaster of St Hugh's School, Oxfordshire, and chairman of the Independent Association of Prep Schools

As a father, my context is revisiting the building blocks of the English language so that I can help my son. I found *Grammatix* an ideal companion, aiding me as much as him. As a sometime writer and lover of words, I found myself gradually enthralled by such an accessible and instructive guide through this somewhat dry but vital base to all things literary. I particularly enjoyed the way in which the pupils had evidently engaged with their teacher to demonstrate the various techniques. I thought this inspirational for my son and totally relevant, as it had clearly been great fun. *Grammatix* has helped me take a fresh look at how I write and how I teach my son to write. I couldn't have enjoyed it more and I will be referring to it regularly – both for him and for me!

Iain Hilleary, parent of a school-age child

Many teachers will find *Grammatix* a useful reference point for checking/building grammar knowledge, and the examples of analyses of real texts will be enormously helpful, as often this is an area of lesser confidence.

Debra Myhill, professor of education, University of Exeter

Sarah has split various skills logically with easy-to-follow explanations, activities and follow-up tasks. There are lots of other texts that have exercises, but these tend to be compartmentalised, whereas Sarah has pulled everything together to show how a focused approach to grammar can lead to great finished pieces of work.

Philip Gibson, assistant head, Davenies School, Buckinghamshire

I like the format of explaining the grammar before asking students to identify and correct it in someone else's writing, then having a go at using it themselves. Our students will really benefit from this book and could easily complete the work independently. The activities are ideal for cover lessons and homework, too.

Emma Stroud, assistant principal for teaching and learning, Harris Academy South Norwood

CONTENTS

FOREWORD

The study of grammar has gone through something of a dark age in recent decades. It is often associated with discussion of error or correctness, but the real reasons for studying grammar appear to have faded from the collective memory. This is perhaps owing to significant changes in the methods of studying grammar, and also to a failure to see its study as a meaningful and delightful pursuit in its own right.

This was not always the case.

During antiquity, the study of grammar was a companion to the study of rhetoric. In the medieval period, it was one of the seven liberal arts. For anyone seeking enlightenment and truth, the study of grammar is of fundamental importance because it gives us the language to talk about language itself. Understanding the nature of language itself shines a light on who we are. That is to say, the study of grammar helps us to know ourselves and others.

A mastery of grammar enables us to sort linguistic fact from linguistic fiction. It reveals the depth in poetry and in the poet; it unlocks the meaning in story and the subterfuge in documentary. We study grammar because we want to be learned; we want to have the mechanisms and tools to take part in the great conversation that is the ascent of humanity. The study of grammar should be central to all models of education.

It is time for grammar to undergo a resurgence in our schools. Achieving such a resurgence will require schools, teachers, pupils and parents to have the best possible guidance. Grammar is based on rules; it is formal yet ever-changing, and of vital importance if we are to thrive in a world so full of information. The study of grammar therefore needs to be rigorous and seen as worthy of effort and interest. This is why *Grammatix* arrives at just the right time.

In this book, Sarah North strikes a perfect balance between rigour and inspiration. She guides pupils and teachers through the foundations of grammar using instruction, exercise and reflection, as well as reference to the real work of her pupils.

The format of *Grammatix* has been carefully planned. Step by step, Sarah helps readers to strengthen their understanding of convention, structure, form and style, while building a love of good writing and a knowledge of what makes a good writer. Teacher and pupil alike will sense Sarah's enjoyment of words and her certainty that, through the study of grammar, their own enjoyment of literature will deepen.

When Sarah first sent this book to me, some friends commented that I was an unusual choice of critic: 'A mathematician!' they protested. But, as a mathematician, I loved reading this book and undertaking the tasks throughout. The structure of grammar in the English language is very much like the structure of grammar in mathematics: the technical detail builds and connects, revealing the true meaning of the subject. It is by knowing the rules as currently stated, and knowing that they are in motion, that one can become meaningfully involved in a subject. I strongly encourage readers to engage with the tasks as they progress through the book. Doing so provides a clear sense of how the technical details combine to form a schema of knowledge that opens up the English language.

As David Crystal reminds us in his book *Making Sense of Grammar*, 'Grammar is the structural foundation of our ability to express ourselves. The more we are aware of how it works, the more we can monitor the meaning and effectiveness of the way we and others use language. It can help foster precision, detect ambiguity, and exploit the richness of expression available in English. And it can help everyone – not only teachers of English but teachers of anything, for all teaching is ultimately a matter of getting to grips with meaning.'

It is, of course, important to be able to understand what sentences mean. But, in these pages, Sarah shows us *how* sentences mean. Her meticulously planned, comprehensive journey through the study of grammar equips the reader – whether they are a teacher, pupil or parent – to get the most out of great writing and to produce great writing themselves. Enjoy.

Mark McCourt, founder of La Salle Education and author of Teaching for Mastery

INTRODUCTION

A principal part of enjoying English is reading books and sharing discussions about characters and how they interact with each other. It's about being gripped by a plot – its moments of drama or those moments when events in a character's experience change them, either for the better or for the worse. Our own recognition of some of the issues experienced by characters is what engages us in books and keeps us reading to find out what happens next.

When writers have succeeded in gripping their readers, it is because of the words they have chosen to put on the page and the way those words are arranged. A writer can make us feel tense and breathless, happy or sad, disappointed or shocked, and good writers are those who instinctively adopt particular techniques to achieve intended effects.

Good writers are those with the ability to craft their ideas using specific sentence types and punctuation to entertain their readers. They know how to create mood and atmosphere through varying the focuses of their paragraphs and they have the power to create characters we want to be with, whose futures we care about and whose trials and tribulations we share.

Successful writers are those who read widely. By exposing themselves to lots of styles and voices, they consciously (and unconsciously) weave them into their own writing.

Grammatix is designed to highlight the ways in which writers achieve their effects and to provide opportunities for emulating their techniques. It's a holistic resource for English mentors (teachers, private tutors and parents) and pupils aged 11-18 who need to understand key aspects of English grammar as stipulated in the national curriculum.

Not only does it explain the theory of grammar but also, step by step, its application for creativity and analysis. The book offers opportunities for individual research and sophisticated vocabulary development, and the chance to see grammar at work across a wide variety of literature. It also contains real and inspirational examples of pupils' work.

Younger pupils may find the work challenging at times, but *Grammatix* is intended to provide strong, comprehensive foundations on which to build, not just in preparation for tests and exams, but also for unlocking and enjoying the enigmatic mysteries and wonders of the English language.

We will explore word classes: nouns, adjectives, verbs, adverbs, pronouns, prepositions, determiners and conjunctions. These are the building blocks of writing. We will consider the patterns and combinations that link the building blocks: the phrases; the subordinate clauses; the main clauses; the simple, compound and complex sentences; the questions; the commands and the exclamations. These form the architectural structure of writing. And we will discuss punctuation: the full stops, commas, exclamation marks, question marks, dialogue punctuation, ellipses, colons and semicolons. These form the vital cement that holds the structures together and they contribute specific meanings of their own.

Grammatix offers a variety of tasks to allow pupils to put what they have learned into practice. Answers or suggested responses are provided in the appendix at the back of the book. Some of the tasks are more creative and could have many possible answers – the point is not for pupils to get the 'right' answer but to understand what the task is trying to teach them.

The final chapter of the book contains ideas to help English mentors develop their pupils' skills of creativity, craftsmanship and analysis.

Grammatix does not purport to be the last and final word on grammar, which is constantly evolving. Certain rules and points of style will always be contested. Nevertheless, if young people are exposed to these techniques they will have a strong base of knowledge. Should they choose to relax the rules as they develop their own style of writing, they can do so from an informed perspective.

FULL STOP!

Sarah North, October 2020

1. NOUNS

VOCABULARY DEVELOPMENT

Complete the grid. For each word, use a dictionary to identify the word class and meaning.

Word	Word class	Meaning
crickets		
demented		
to attain		
to stomp		
an array		
statistician		
busker		
Camembert		

IN THIS CHAPTER WE WILL COVER:

- Noun categories.
- Definite/indefinite article and determiners.
- Structuring analytical responses.
- Using precise nouns and their contribution to mood, atmosphere and setting.

NOUNS ARE NAMING WORDS

They name things (**common nouns**), countries/towns/cities and people (**proper nouns**), groups of things (**collective nouns**) and ideas (**abstract nouns**).

Common nouns

Desk, chair, window, nose.

Proper nouns

There are various types of proper noun. All use capital letters.

- **Places**: Faringdon, Oxford, Italy, India, Africa.
- **Nationalities and languages**: English, Turkish, French.
- **Known events**: World War II, Christmas Eve.
- **People**: Bill Gates, Michelle Obama, Lord Lucan, Mum (if that is your name for her) but 'my mum' if you are referring to her. A capital letter is often used for the Prime Minister/the President/the Headteacher (if we are referring specifically to the person and their title). But lower case is used if we are referring to prime ministers, presidents or headteachers in general.

Collective nouns

A **herd** of cattle, a **gaggle** of geese, a **crowd** of people.

Note that although collective nouns refer to a group of things, we regard them as singular, not plural:

> The crowd **is** moving this way.
> The herd **is** out of control.

Abstract nouns

Knowledge, wisdom, tomorrow, hunger.

These are ideas that you can't touch (they are intangible).

Abstract nouns are not to be confused with 'untouchable' common nouns like 'air' or 'mist'.

Definite and indefinite articles

Definite and indefinite articles work with nouns to define them.

- Definite article: **the**. The trees, the families, the ambulances.
- Indefinite article: **a/an**. A tree, a family, an ambulance. 'An' is the same as 'a' but is used before a noun beginning with a vowel (a, e, i, o, u). 'An' is also sometimes used before a noun beginning with an aspirate (silent) 'h'.

It is not always necessary to use the definite article in front of nouns and overuse of 'the' can clutter our writing. For example:

> *The people clung to each other and **the** queues of **the** elderly, **the** middle-aged, **the** children, **the** toddlers and **the** babies (in assorted prams) stretched for what seemed to be miles.*

might flow better as:

> *People clung to each other and queues of the elderly, the middle-aged, children, toddlers and babies (in assorted prams) stretched for what seemed to be miles.*

Determiners

Sometimes people will refer to the definite and indefinite articles as 'determiners'. A determiner is a word that introduces a noun (such as a/an, the) but the term can also refer to other words that describe or introduce nouns (such as 'every', 'some', 'this', 'that').

TASK 1

Read the following passage and underline the nouns. Label each one as common, proper, collective or abstract. The first three have been done for you.

             common   *common*   *common*
The midday <u>sun</u> burnt the back of her <u>legs</u> and the <u>crickets</u> in the French

countryside sounded like a demented gaggle of geese. She wanted to swim

in the pool but her English homework beckoned and, as her mum kept telling

her, knowledge was not inherited but attained through hard work. She had

been threatened with poor reports from the Headmaster but even this couldn't

persuade her that swimming was not a preferable option to studying nouns.

Caroline sighed. Her brother stomped past carrying an array of swimming pool

gear. From behind his mask, he smirked at her and, though he was already

wearing his snorkel, she made out his words: 'You're being watched. A crowd of

headmasters is coming for you.' World War III was about to erupt.

TASK 2

Read the following passage:

> On the last day of term, pupils traditionally played a game called 'Round and Round the Room'. They had to circle the sports hall and back without once touching the floor and they did it by means of wall bars, a vault, a climbing frame and ropes. Anyone who touched the floor with a toe was out and the winner was the pupil who did it in the fastest time.

What is the setting of this passage? Give reasons for your answer.

_____

_____

_____

_____

TASK 3

Read the following passage:

> On the last night of the skiing holiday, our two families played a game called 'Hunt the Camembert'. You had to hide the cheese somewhere in the chalet and wear your ski clothes – helmet, ski suit, moon boots and gloves – to find it. The helmet was covered with a ski scarf and the winner was the person who found the Camembert in the fastest time.

What is the setting of this passage? Give reasons for your answer.

_____

_____

_____

_____

From your answers and discussions, you will understand that _precise_ nouns are vital for creating settings.

TASK 4

A class of pupils created a list of nouns associated with the setting **The High Street**, which they incorporated into one piece of writing.

Their nouns:

> shops, pedestrians, statistician, buses, cars, taxis, cyclists,
> buskers, prams, pub, burger bar, lamp post, bin.

William, a pupil, wrote this piece entitled 'The High Street':

The blacked out windows stood out intriguingly amongst a tattered row of shops. As scattered pedestrians bustled their way through, a statistician, holding a clipboard, could easily be seen standing next to the traffic lights - What was he counting? Busses, cars, taxis, cyclists? The evening light was fading, as buskers slowly packed away their guitars. Everything seemed normal; mothers pushing prams, the pub and burger bar starting to welcome the evening trade ... but was it?

Suddenly, a tumultuous roar could be heard coming from the shop with the blacked out windows as two men, who had the disgruntled appearance of beggars, flung open the door and ran towards the tube station. One was bleeding profusely. As people fled, the beeps of the zebra crossing could still be heard. The lamppost lamppost flickered as the police sirens blared. Ominously the statistician was nowhere to be seen as smoke billowed from a bin on the other side of the street.

Now it's your turn. Write a list of nouns (around 15-20) appropriate for the setting **The Harbour**.

In the space below, write a piece entitled 'The Harbour' that uses *all* the nouns you have gathered. Underline or highlight your nouns.

2. ADJECTIVES

VOCABULARY DEVELOPMENT

Complete the grid. For each word, use a dictionary to identify the word class and meaning.

Word	Word class	Meaning
poplars		
doddery		
bespectacled		
cobbled		
explicit		
vague		
writhing		
mogul field		
hysterical		
landmark		
frenzy		
competent		
composed		
irascible		
timid		
indignant		
effusive		
hyperbolic		
obsequious		

IN THIS CHAPTER WE WILL COVER:

- Types of adjective.
- Homophones and the difference between possessive adjectives and apostrophes for possession.
- Recognising the effects of precise adjectives.

ADJECTIVES DESCRIBE NOUNS

There are various types of adjective: **descriptive**, **demonstrative**, **interrogative**, **possessive**, **comparative** and **superlative**.

Descriptive adjectives

These adjectives describe nouns. They provide extra detail and serve to bring the pictures we are trying to create into sharper focus.

We need to be careful not to overuse adjectives. First and foremost, it is important to find a precise noun rather than fling a lot of adjectives at a nondescript noun. The following examples are not incorrect but they are examples of weak writing:

> *The big, old, ancient, towering tree.*
>
> *The wrinkled, dull, old man.*
>
> *The tireless, never-ending road.*

Think about the **nouns** used in those examples. How can we make them more precise? Is the tree an oak, a holly, a sycamore, a poplar? Is the man a farmer, a police officer, a grandfather? Is the road a lane, a motorway, an alley?

And now think of just one or two thoughtful **adjectives** to add to the precise noun:

> *The **rustling** poplars.*
>
> *The **doddery, bespectacled** grandfather.*
>
> *The **cobbled** alleyway.*

Demonstrative adjectives

This, that, those (also known as determiners). These adjectives are used alongside nouns to draw attention or to demonstrate a particular noun:

> ***This** pen.*
>
> ***Those** chairs.*
>
> ***That** projector.*

Interrogative adjectives

Which, whose, what (also known as determiners). These adjectives are used alongside nouns to ask a question or to interrogate:

> ***Which** pen belongs to you?*
>
> ***Whose** chairs are those?*
>
> ***What** cheese would you like?*

Possessive adjectives

My, your, his/her/its, our, your (plural), their.

	Singular	Plural
First person	my pen	our pen
Second person	your pen	your (plural) pen
Third person	his pen her pen its pen	their pen

Homophones are words that have the same pronunciation but have different meanings or spellings. The word 'homophone' comes from the Greek *homos* (same) and *phone* (sound).

Common homophones include:

- **Its** – possessive adjective.
- **It's** – a contraction of two words, 'it is', using an apostrophe.
- **Their** – possessive adjective.
- **They're** – a contraction of two words, 'they are', using an apostrophe.

The possessive adjectives 'its' and 'their' do not have an apostrophe as they are a unit in their own right. We would not be tempted to put an apostrophe in the middle of other possessive adjectives, such as 'my' or 'our', so we do not need to put an apostrophe in the middle of 'its' or 'their' if they are working as possessive adjectives.

Comparative and superlative adjectives

A **comparative** adjective works alongside a noun to make a comparison or to compare:

> He is wearing **cleaner** shoes now.
> They are using **brighter** colours in their paintings.
> Her work is **harder** than yours.

A **superlative** adjective gives the noun it works with the highest status:

> He is wearing the **cleanest** shoes in the class.
> They are using the **brightest** colours in their paintings.
> Her work is the **hardest** to do.

It seems from these examples that comparative and superlative adjectives are formed by adding -er or -est (respectively) to a descriptive adjective:

Descriptive adjective	Comparative adjective	Superlative adjective
clean	cleaner	cleanest
bright	brighter	brightest
hard	harder	hardest

This is often the case, but below are some exceptions:

Descriptive adjective	Comparative adjective	Superlative adjective
good	better	best
competitive	more competitive	most competitive
beautiful	more beautiful	most beautiful

Deciding on the correct one can be tricky and is a case of developing an ear for standard English, as opposed to non-standard English. Here are some examples of non-standard English:

> You are gooder than she is.
>
> She is beautifuller than her sister.
>
> She is the most competitivist person I know.

Adjectives have various effects on passages of writing. Sometimes writers will deliberately use comparative or superlative adjectives incorrectly to convey the words of a little child or someone for whom English is not a fully mastered second language:

> It's not fair. She didn't give me the bestest present.
>
> Excuse me. Where is the most nearest petrol station?

TASK 1A

Underline the **nouns** in the following extract from *The Tale of Tom Kitten* by Beatrix Potter.

> *Mrs Tabitha dressed Moppet and Mittens in clean pinafores and tuckers and then she took out all sorts of elegant, uncomfortable clothes.*

TASK 1B

Now underline the **adjectives**.

> *Mrs Tabitha dressed Moppet and Mittens in clean pinafores and tuckers and then she took out all sorts of elegant, uncomfortable clothes.*

TASK 1C

What type of adjectives are used in the Beatrix Potter extract? Are they descriptive, demonstrative, interrogative, possessive or comparative/superlative?

Answer:

The adjectives used in this passage are examples of _____ adjectives.

What effect does the precise use of nouns and adjectives have on the passage?

Answer:

The precise use of nouns and adjectives creates a _____ picture.

TASK 2A

Underline the demonstrative adjectives in the following passage:

First, Mrs Meldrew gathered some shells into her hand. 'These shells came from a beach on an uninhabited island in Italy. Help yourself to these shells, those pencils by the window and that coloured paper on my desk. With this picture as our inspiration, we are going to create a collage using the white glue in that cupboard under the sink.'

TASK 2B

From this short passage, we have gleaned that Mrs Meldrew is a teacher who prefers to give explicit instructions. This is apparent from her clear use of demonstrative adjectives.

In the space below, list the demonstrative adjectives used in the passage. To develop your skill at 'embedding quotations' within your answers, remember to pick out examples or quotations within inverted commas ('……….').

_____

_____

TASK 3A

Underline the interrogative adjectives in the passage below:

'I can't hold it,' shrieked Mandy as she wrestled with the boat's helm.

The sails were writhing in the Force 8 gale and the sailing boat was pitching and tossing in the watery mogul field of waves. Mandy was hysterical. Questions flew from her as she struggled to retain her balance. 'Which rope should I pull? What landmark should I follow? Whose charts must I use?'

But it was no use. Her voice was lost in the frenzy of noise.

TASK 3B

In what frame of mind is Mandy? Underline the appropriate options and complete the sentence:

Mandy seems to be **a/an competent/inexperienced** and **panic-stricken/**

composed sailor. This is apparent from the number of times Mandy uses

interrogative adjectives such as _____, _____

and _____.

TASK 4

Read the following passage and underline the correct options:

'**Its/It's** unfair. **It's/Its** my kitchen, not **hi's/his** and these are **m'y/my** things, not **your/you're** things. I want my house back!'

She flung the door back and stomped along the corridor. He could hear her muttering, 'These people are invading my space with **they're/their** clutter and mess.'

Choose the word/words which best describe the character speaking in the passage:

☐ Irascible   ☐ Frightened   ☐ Possessive   ☐ Timid

How has the writer achieved this effect? Count the number of times the writer has used the possessive adjective 'my':

_____

The writer has achieved this effect by _____

_____

_____

_____

_____

_____

_____

TASK 5

Read the following letter:

Castle Close

Steventon

Oxon

5th August

Dear Mrs Brown,

Thank you for providing us with the most delicious lunch yesterday. The pizza was the spiciest I've ever eaten and the ice cream was the coldest. You are a far more competent cook than I could ever be.

The sea views from your house are the most spectacular I've ever seen.

Thank you for having me. I had a much better time with you than being at home.

Kindest regards,

Christine

Choose the word/words which best describe the tone of this letter:

☐ Critical   ☐ Indignant   ☐ Hesitant   ☐ Effusive   ☐ Hyperbolic

Complete the following statement using examples from the letter and appropriate words selected from this list:

obsequious	possessive	sincere	demonstrative
interrogative	exaggerated	superlative	appreciation
distaste	descriptive	insincere	effusive

The extensive use of _____ adjectives such as _____

_____ and the

use of comparative adjectives such as _____ and _____ convey

an impression of Christine's _____ for the lunch she had at Mrs Brown's house.

However, the tone of the letter is so _____ that it is in danger of sounding

_____ and _____ .

3. VERBS

VOCABULARY DEVELOPMENT

Complete the grid. For each word, use a dictionary to identify the word class and meaning.

Word	Word class	Meaning
vigorous		
toddler		
carrier		
seldom		
rockery		
pinafore		
deferential		
diplomatic		
intimidated		
enthralled		
invigorated		
staccato		
elusive		
britches		
putty		
chrysanthemums		
elms		
sobriety		
to hoard		
conformist	adjective	
defiant		
eccentric	adjective	
conventional		

IN THIS CHAPTER WE WILL COVER:

- Identifying verbs and their contribution to mood.
- Transitive and intransitive verbs.
- Using adjectives and verbs to bring settings/mood into sharper focus.
- Key terminology associated with verbs.
- First-, second- and third-person narrative.
- Passive and active voice.
- Verb tenses.
- Auxiliary verbs/participles/modal verbs.
- Poetry analysis (the effects of verbs).
- Emulating structural techniques and experimenting with verbs.

VERBS ARE 'DOING' OR 'BEING' WORDS

Sentences are not sentences without verbs; verbs bring sense to a group of words.

> She **sighed** in the classroom.
>
> We **howled** in despair and **stamped** our feet on the cobbles.

Transitive and intransitive verbs

Transitive verbs require an object to make sense:

Subject	Transitive verb	Object
Ade	loves	chocolate cake

Intransitive verbs *do not* require an object to make sense:

Subject	Intransitive verb
Rajiv	gasped
Lyra	laughed

Because verbs are described as 'doing' words, we often feel we need to bring life to our writing by using vigorous verbs. This is quite right, but inexperienced writers often feel they need to ensure that all their characters are doing 'vigorous' things like 'sprinting', 'skipping' and 'leaping'.

As with our choice of nouns and adjectives, the key to creating the right picture is to select the *precise* verb for the job. We rarely 'sprint' unless we are running the 100m, yet developing writers might have their characters 'sprinting' downstairs or 'sprinting' into the car. Characters might 'jump' into their clothes or 'trundle' or 'trudge' everywhere, or 'sweat' buckets at the first sign of tension.

In the passage below, the character does not sprint – far from it – and yet the verbs are vigorous because they convey a consistent picture of disconsolance.

> I **dragged** myself downstairs, **mumbled** 'Morning' to my mum as she **stirred** the
>
> porridge, and **slumped** into a kitchen chair.

Take this sentence:

She went down the road.

The picture is limited because the word choices are imprecise. If we swap 'she' for 'the toddler', 'went' for 'waddled' and 'road' for 'concrete', we create a much more specific picture without any need for an adjective:

The toddler waddled across the concrete.

Completely different pictures are created in the following examples:

Soldiers limped from the battlefield.
The farmer ploughed his fields last week.

We can choose to bring the picture into sharper focus by introducing some adjectives:

*The **sobbing** toddler waddled across the **frozen** concrete.*
***Injured** soldiers limped from the **water-logged** battlefield.*
*The **red-faced** farmer ploughed his **west-facing** fields last week.*

The infinitive

The basic form of a verb is known as an infinitive: to go, to swim, to eat, to be, to have, to smile, etc. In French (and other languages), the infinitive is only one word:

English	French	Italian	German
To go	aller	andare	gehen
To swim	nager	nuotare	schwimmen
To eat	manger	mangiare	essen
To be	être	essere	sein
To have	avoir	avere	haben
To smile	sourire	sorridere	lächeln

In English, the infinitive is nearly always accompanied by the preposition 'to', but there are exceptions which are known as 'bare infinitives'. For example:

To go: *She bade him go.*

To sit: *Kwame let Bella sit in his chair.*

To cry: *Harry made Mei cry.*

To sing: *I heard him sing in the concert.*

Verb tenses

Verbs are put into various tenses to convey present or past.

Present tense		
	Singular	**Plural**
First person	I eat	We eat
Second person	You eat	You (plural) eat
Third person	He/she/it eats	They eat

Simple past tense		
	Singular	**Plural**
First person	I ate	We ate
Second person	You ate	You (plural) ate
Third person	He/she/it ate	They ate

The most common ways of expressing the future in English are to use 'will' (to express prediction) or 'going to' (to express intention).

Future tense		
	Singular	**Plural**
First person	I will eat I am going to eat	We will eat We are going to eat
Second person	You will eat You are going to eat	You (plural) will eat/You (plural) are going to eat
Third person	He/she/it will eat He/she/it is going to eat	They will eat They are going to eat

Some people argue that there is no future tense in English, because the verb form does not change. They say that what we describe as a future tense is actually just the present tense with future meaning. Despite this, as it still *functions* as a future tense, we will refer to it as the 'future tense' here.

First-person narrative and past tense

Autobiographies and diaries are written in the first-person narrative: I (singular) or we (plural). This gives readers the chance to experience, first-hand, the writer's thoughts and feelings:

Although I tried to brazen it out, inside I was dying with embarrassment and shame.

Thoughts shrieked in my head and I struggled to keep control over the lump that

was blocking my throat and my chin which was threatening to wobble. I scrabbled for

something dignified to say.

The past tense is used for diaries and autobiographies as events have already occurred.

TASK 1

This is the opening sentence from Laurie Lee's autobiography, *Cider with Rosie*:

> *I was set down from the carrier's cart at the age of three; and there with a sense of bewilderment and terror my life in the village began.*

Copy the sentence down, underlining the verbs and writing the infinitive in brackets after each verb.

_____

_____

_____

_____

_____

Second-person narrative

The second-person narrative is seldom used other than for instructions:

> **You** *will need three reading books, two exercise books and one pen.*
> **You** *must bring all these things to your lessons.*

But, sometimes, writers will also use 'you' in order to avoid using the very formal 'one':

> *At school,* **you** *can choose your own tutor.*

In instances such as this, it would be more correct for the writer to use the passive voice instead of 'you':

> *At school, tutors can be chosen by pupils.*

Active and passive voice

The passive voice is used when writers want to write objectively as opposed to subjectively. When the active voice is turned into the passive voice, the subject and object switch places. For example:

- **Active voice:** *Jane requested tea.*
  Jane is the subject, 'requested' is the verb, tea is the object.

- **Passive voice:** *Tea was requested by Jane.*
  Tea is the subject, 'requested' is the verb, Jane is the object.

Here are some other examples:

Active voice	Passive voice
The Labrador bit the child	The child was bitten by the Labrador
The grill burnt my hand	My hand was burnt by the grill
Ollie cleaned the kitchen	The kitchen was cleaned by Ollie

This technique is used for formal contexts such as report writing or text books. In a formal context such as a travel brochure, it would be common and correct to write:

1. *From the upstairs windows of the apartment, the Eiffel Tower can be seen.*

Or in a police or newspaper report:

2. *An elderly lady was robbed by three unemployed youths last Friday.*

Or, if the identity of someone is being withheld:

3. *The classroom door has been broken.*

TASK 2

Convert the passive voice in the three sentences above into the active voice.

1. _____

_____

2. _____

_____

3. _____

_____

Third-person narrative

The third person (he/she/it, they) is used in many fictional books. Here is another passage from *The Tale of Tom Kitten* by Beatrix Potter, written in the third person:

> *Tom Kitten was quite unable to jump when walking upon his hind legs in trousers. He came up the rockery by degrees, breaking the ferns and shedding buttons right and left.*

TASK 3

Read the following extract from *The Tale of Tom Kitten* and underline the verbs.

> *Moppet and Mittens walked down the garden path unsteadily. Presently, they trod upon their pinafores and fell on their noses. When they stood up, there were several green smears.*

Which tense is this extract written in?

The extract is written in the _____ tense.

TASK 4

I have listed the verbs used in the extract. Alongside each one, write the infinitive and convert each verb into the present and the future. The first one has been done for you.

Verb	Infinitive	Present tense	Future tense
walked	to walk	they walk	they will walk
trod			
fell			
stood up			
were			

The present tense

The most common tense used in fiction is the past tense, but sometimes writers will use the present tense. The present tense suggests that the outcome is not yet known but is happening in real time, so it can have the effect of creating a sense of immediacy and unresolved excitement:

> *Priya walks into the dining hall and immediately senses discomfort. People aren't staring exactly but there is a stillness about them, an air of frozen expectancy. Priya affects a relaxed sense of ease which she is far from feeling.*

The future tense

I will/I am going to.

The future tense can create a sense of dominance and control over another character:

> Tomorrow, you will do exactly as I tell you. You will walk to the post office without stopping. You will collect a brown parcel addressed to Rufus Redcliffe and then you will go to the café in the corner of the Square. Order a 'flat white' and wait. You will receive a call on your mobile phone with further instructions.

The future tense is also an effective device in persuasive writing, such as a charity appeal, as it can suggest that the reader has already been partially persuaded:

> By giving just £10 a month, you'll [**a contraction of 'you will'**] be providing shelter for three homeless children and enough food and water to sustain 10 children for a year. You'll never regret your decision to help.

The imperative mood

The imperative mood is used in persuasive writing to inject a sense of urgency or to call out to the reader, engaging her/his attention:

> Act now! Give generously today to save lives!

Infinitive	Imperative
To buy	Buy one today!
To go	Go now!
To eat	Eat it!

TASK 5

Tick the word you feel is most appropriate to complete the sentence.

A character who fires imperatives/commands at other people would be considered:

☐ Deferential   ☐ Diplomatic   ☐ Authoritative   ☐ Insecure

People who bark imperatives can make others feel:

☐ Fascinated   ☐ Intimidated   ☐ Enthralled   ☐ Invigorated

TASK 6A

Read the poem *Pigeons* by Richard Kell.

They paddle with staccato feet
In powder-pools of sunlight,
Small blue busybodies
Strutting like fat gentlemen
With hands clasped
Under their swallowtail coats;
And, as they stump about,
Their heads like tiny hammers
Tap at imaginary nails
In non-existent walls.

Elusive ghosts of sunshine
Slither down the green gloss
Of their necks in an instant, and are gone.

Summer hangs drugged from sky to earth
In limpid fathoms of silence:
Only warm dark dimples of sound
Slide like slow bubbles
From the contented throats.
Raise a casual hand – with one quick gust
They fountain into air.

What is the poem about?

_____

_____

_____

_____

_____

_____

TASK 6B

What, specifically, are the first, second and third verses/stanzas about?

TASK 6C

Focus on the first verse/stanza. Underline any verbs which describe the pigeons. Make a list of the verbs used in the table below and write the infinitive of each verb.

The first one has been done for you. As the verb is a quotation from the poem, remember to put inverted commas around it.

	Verb	Infinitive
1	'paddle'	to paddle
2		
3		
4		
5		

TASK 6D

From the verbs used in verse/stanza 1, what impression do you receive of the pigeons?

In your answer, use specific **adjectives** to describe the 'impression' you have received of the pigeons and give reasons. Notice also the syllables in each of the verbs used to describe the pigeons' movements. Think about the effect this has on the types of movements you imagine the pigeons to be making.

From the verbs used in verse/stanza 1, I have the impression that the pigeons are _____

_____

_____

_____

_____

_____

_____

Participles – present and past

Every verb has a present and past participle:

Infinitive	Present tense	Past tense	Present participle	Past participle
To walk	(she) walks	(she) walked	…walking	…walked
To teach	(she) teaches	(she) taught	…teaching	…taught
To cry	(she) cries	(she) cried	…crying	…cried
To mumble	(she) mumbles	(she) mumbled	…mumbling	…mumbled

From the table above, you will notice that all present participles end in -ing. This is the case *always*. You might also think that past participles look exactly the same as the past tense. In these regular verbs, they do, but there are exceptions. Here are some of them:

Infinitive	Present tense	Past tense	Present participle	Past participle
To sing	(she) sings	(she) **sang**	…singing	…**sung**
To eat	(she) eats	(she) **ate**	…eating	…**eaten**
To have	(she) has	(she) **had**	…having	…**had**
To be	(she) is	(she) **was**	…being	…**been**
To swim	(she) swims	(she) **swam**	…swimming	…**swum**

Present and past participles provide us with flexibility but, within a sentence, they need to be supported by an **auxiliary verb** (also known as a helping verb). This is why, in the tables above, each example has been preceded by an ellipsis (…).

The word 'auxiliary', meaning assistant or helper, comes from the Latin *auxilium* (help). The primary auxiliary verbs in English are **be**, **do** and **have**.

A group of words containing just present or past participles cannot work. For example:

> *She walking to the shops.*

So we need to add an auxiliary verb:

> She **is/was/will be/has been** *walking to the shops.*

'Is', 'was', 'will be' and 'has been' are all examples of auxiliary verbs.

TASK 7

Convert the following groups of words into sentences by adding auxiliary verbs to the past participles:

She eaten by sharks.   She _____ eaten by sharks.

She swum around the rocks.   She _____ swum around the rocks.

She been on holiday.   She _____ been on holiday.

People frequently – and incorrectly – use the past participle 'sat' or 'stood' with an auxiliary verb:

I am sat/I was sat/I was stood.

In this instance, the **present participle** with the **auxiliary verb** is the correct version:

I am sitting/I was sitting/I am standing/I was standing.

TASK 8A

Read the poem *Child on Top of a Greenhouse* by Theodore Roethke.

The wind billowing out the seat of my britches,
My feet crackling splinters of glass and dried putty,
The half-grown chrysanthemums staring up like accusers,
Up through the streaked glass, flashing with sunlight,
A few white clouds all rushing eastward,
A line of elms plunging and tossing like horses,
And everyone, everyone pointing up and shouting!

What is the poem about?

_____

_____

_____

_____

TASK 8B

How does the title make you feel? How has this been achieved?

TASK 8C

Underline the nouns in the poem. What clues do the nouns provide regarding setting and atmosphere (weather, etc)?

TASK 8D

Who is the speaker in the poem? How does the speaker feel? Give reasons for your answer.

With questions of this sort, there can be various interpretations and any might be acceptable so long as they are clearly supported with explanations and evidence.

_____

_____

_____

_____

_____

_____

TASK 8E

Now underline the present participles.

> *The wind billowing out the seat of my britches,*
>
> *My feet crackling splinters of glass and dried putty,*
>
> *The half-grown chrysanthemums staring up like accusers,*
>
> *Up through the streaked glass, flashing with sunlight,*
>
> *A few white clouds all rushing eastward,*
>
> *A line of elms plunging and tossing like horses,*
>
> *And everyone, everyone pointing up and shouting!*

In poetry, poets can write in a way which might be considered inaccurate in terms of **syntax** (the way words and phrases are arranged to form well-constructed sentences) among those who write **prose** (written or spoken language in its ordinary form, without poetic structure). This is because most poets are writing 'condensed', multi-layered versions of prose to increase poetic impact.

TASK 8F

Rewrite Roethke's poem as a paragraph of prose. Use the auxiliary verb 'to be' to improve the syntax and underline the instances you use.

I will write the first line for you:

The wind is billowing out the seat of my britches.

I could also choose **was** or **will be**. Whichever tense you choose for your auxiliary verbs, you must be consistent all the way through.

Modal verbs

Can, could, may, might, must, shall, should not and would.

Modal verbs are close relations of auxiliary verbs. They serve to contribute flexibility and meaning to other verbs. They can suggest possibility and certainty:

> *She **might be** arriving in time for supper (**possibility**).*
> *She **will be** arriving in time for supper (**certainty**).*

TASK 9

Underline the participles in the following sentences. In the brackets after each sentence, write whether the participle is present or past (remember all present participles end in -ing). Highlight the modal verbs and write them in the brackets also.

The first one has been done for you:

> *She may have eaten contaminated food.*
>
> *(past participle = eaten; modal verbs = may, have)*

They must have arrived by now.

(_____)

I shall be doing all I can to sort things out.

(_____)

She should not have spoken to me like that.

(_____)

Uses of the verbs 'to be' or 'to have' with either the present participle or the past participle of a verb are known, more formally, as the following:

- **Present progressive**: she is eating.
- **Future progressive**: she will be eating.
- **Imperfect**: she was eating.
- **Present perfect**: she has eaten.
- **Past perfect** (known in French and Latin as the pluperfect): she had eaten.
- **Future perfect**: she will have eaten.
- **Past perfect progressive**: she had been eating.

There are also such constructions as the future perfect progressive (she will have been eating) and present perfect progressive (she has been eating) and there are many other combinations. Most of them will be used fluently and accurately by accomplished English speakers without there being any need for identifying them specifically, unless studying for SATs or learning a foreign language at an advanced level.

Verbs in context and their effects

In Jenny Joseph's poem *Warning*, the poet wants to warn everyone that when she is old, she will not be a typical old lady.

When I am an old woman I shall wear purple

With a red hat which doesn't go, and doesn't suit me.

And I shall spend my pension on brandy and summer gloves

And satin sandals, and say we've no money for butter.

I shall sit down on the pavement when I'm tired

And gobble up samples in shops and press alarm bells

And run my stick along the public railings

And make up for the sobriety of my youth.

I shall go out in my slippers in the rain

And pick flowers in other people's gardens

And learn to spit.

You can wear terrible shirts and grow more fat

And eat three pounds of sausages at a go

Or only bread and pickle for a week

And hoard pens and pencils and beermats and things in boxes.

But now we must have clothes that keep us dry

And pay our rent and not swear in the street

And set a good example for the children.

We must have friends to dinner and read the papers.

But maybe I ought to practise a little now?

So people who know me are not too shocked and surprised

When suddenly I am old, and start to wear purple.

TASK 10A

Tick the adjectives you feel appropriately describe the poet's attitude.

☐ Conformist   ☐ Angry   ☐ Miserable   ☐ Joyful   ☐ Defiant   ☐ Eccentric

TASK 10B

Why do you think the poem is called 'Warning'?

_____

_____

_____

_____

_____

_____

_____

TASK 10C

On the poem, underline how many times Joseph uses the modal auxiliary 'shall', 'must', 'can' and 'ought' alongside another verb. Think about what these contribute to the tone of her voice.

Now write an adjective which best describes the tone of the following statements:

- I might do the high jump – _____

- I can do the high jump – _____

- I shall do the high jump – _____

Answering analytical questions

Let's consider the following question that might appear on an exam paper:

What impression do you receive of the speaker in the poem? (6 marks)

Here is one possible answer:

I have received various impressions of Jenny Joseph. First of all, she seems defiant as she repeatedly uses the modal verb 'shall' – 'I shall wear purple', 'I shall spend my pension', 'I shall sit down', 'I shall go out in my slippers'. This suggests an emphatic, decisive tone of voice.

The choice of nouns – 'brandy', 'summer gloves', 'satin sandals' – suggests that this 'old woman' retains an unexpected delight in extravagant luxuries.

The choice of verbs – 'gobble up', 'spit' and 'hoard' – suggests the actions of an unruly youth rather than an elderly lady. Jenny Joseph sounds as if she has a sense of humour and that she enjoys shocking and surprising people by not conforming to type.

Note how the writer sets the answer up with an opening statement: 'I have received various impressions of Jenny Joseph.' This lets the marker know that a series of points are going to be made and it has a settling effect on the writer.

As a general rule of thumb, an analytical question of this nature must be answered with a series of points, each supported with an example (quotation) and an explanation which is relevant to the question. In this instance, six marks are available and three points have been made.

PEE (point, example, explanation) is often suggested as a way of structuring an answer to an analytical question. Although considered by some to be formulaic, it is a sound starting point for ensuring that your answers are relevant, systematic, clearly explained and well supported with evidence.

TASK 10D

In the table below, identify the examples and explanations used by the writer to support the three points or impressions.

The first one has been done for you.

Point (impression of the speaker)	Example(s)	Explanation	Marks 6
Defiant	'I shall wear purple'; 'I shall spend my pension'; 'I shall sit down'; 'I shall go out in my slippers'	The use of modal verbs suggests an emphatic and defiant tone	2
			2
			2

TASK 11

For this creative writing task, write a piece of prose entitled either 'Conventional Old Age' or 'Unconventional Old Age'.

Emulate the structure and areas of focus in Jenny Joseph's poem, exploring ideas of your own. See below for examples of other pupils' work.

'CONVENTIONAL OLD AGE', BY TARQUIN

When I am an old man, I shall wear a tweed suit with sensible shoes and a grey top hat. And I shall spend my money on my weekly shop which will include spam, some pipe tobacco and a bottle of Scotch.

When I'm tired, I shall sit in my worn leather armchair and read *The Times*. I shall go out and walk my Jack Russell and learn to take money from one of those funny holes in the wall.

When I'm old I will eat meat and two veg followed by a huge helping of spotted dick and custard.

But for now, I am going to go crazy and live life! I am going to sing out loud, loiter in the street and place a bet on the horses. I will wear a floppy, striped hat which is too big for me.

'UNCONVENTIONAL OLD AGE', BY MILLIE

When I am old, I shall wear snakeskin boots and bright, rainbow colours. When I feel like it, I shall wear fluffy slippers and wellington boots and put on fake eyelashes.

I shall spend my money on graphic movies and confusing gadgets and buy old antiques from dodgy shops.

When I am tired, I will lie down where I am in my clothes and fall asleep. I will call 999 and tell them it's an emergency because I am so tired.

I will go to the shops in my dressing gown and slippers and smash neighbour's windows. I shall kick others' cats and dye my hair green. I will hoard pink paperclips, not the plain ones, and call people rude names.

When I am hungry, I shall eat fish and chips and drink fizzy drinks. I will gobble up my secret stash of lemon sherbets to make my teeth rotten and bad.

But maybe I ought to practise a little now. After all, I'm utterly bored of my current duties. I'm bored of having to pay taxes and visit distant friends. Bored of having to go to work and helping the village community.

It wouldn't hurt if I could try a few things now, as when I am old, I shall wear snakeskin boots and bright, rainbow colours.

Now that you have learnt about nouns, adjectives and verbs, you are beginning to understand how writers' precise use of language creates different effects. You are learning to analyse how language (words/diction) contribute to mood, atmosphere and characterisation.

You can also begin to understand how language is flexible:

Verbs (infinitives)	Adjectives	Nouns
to describe	descriptive	description
to interrogate	interrogative	interrogation
to demonstrate	demonstrative	demonstration
to possess	possessive	possession
to argue	argumentative	argument
to joke	joking/jocular (Wordsworth's poem *Daffodils* uses 'jocund'!)	joke

TASK 12

Complete the following table:

Verbs (infinitives)	Adjectives	Nouns
to lose		loss
	knowing/knowledgeable	
to help	helpful/helping	help
to predict		
	abandoned	
to be wise		wisdom
to run	runny/running	
	recurring	

TASK 13

Underline the verbs in the following passage:

> *The rustling leaves were shimmering in the evening breeze and, having recovered*
> *from being in the losing team, Maya's rate of breathing eased.*

From this exercise, you will understand that words ending in -ing aren't always present participles (verbs). Sometimes they act as adjectives or as nouns:

>   *verb*   *noun*
> *As she was lying in the grass, she contemplated the lying she had witnessed and*
>
>   *adjective*
> *the lying culprit responsible for it. She had suspected Liam to be a liar all along.*

TASK 14

Write a few lines of your own prose, using the present participle as a verb with an auxiliary verb (e.g. she **was lying**), as an adjective (the **lying** culprit) and as a noun (the **lying**). Try to link your ideas as shown above.

_____

_____

_____

_____

_____

_____

Speaking and writing in standard English becomes instinctive for those who read widely and converse with people whose use of the English language is accurate.

- When our use of *spoken* grammar is accurate, we are described as being '**articulate**'.
- When our *writing* is correctly constructed so that it makes complete sense to those reading it, we are described as using correct '**syntax**'.

4. ADVERBS

VOCABULARY DEVELOPMENT

Complete the grid. For each word, use a dictionary to identify the word class and meaning.

Word	Word class	Meaning
tentatively		
collaboratively		
categorically		
gingerly		
surreptitiously		
to deploy		
regional		

IN THIS CHAPTER WE WILL COVER:

- Adverbs and their effects.
- Experimenting with the use and position of adverbs.

IF ADJECTIVES DESCRIBE NOUNS, ADVERBS DESCRIBE VERBS

The clue is in the word itself, adverbs, although they can also say more about an adjective, another adverb or a clause.

> She slept **restlessly**.

> I rode my bike **unsteadily**.

> **Tentatively**, I peeled open the envelope.

> **Happily**, she agreed to marry him.

Not all adverbs end in 'ly':

> I will leave **soon**.

> She works **well**.

Adverbs can be said, therefore, to bring more detail regarding time (I will leave **soon**) and manner (She works **well**) to a sentence.

Beginning a sentence with an adverb (known as 'fronting') can inject a sense of pace and variety to writing. 'Suddenly, the door flew open' has greater dramatic impact than 'The door flew open suddenly' because readers focus most on the first word in the sentence.

When 'fronting', note that a comma is used to separate the adverb or adverbial phrase from the rest of the sentence. But this is not necessary if the adverb appears at the end of the sentence:

> **Slowly but surely**, *she is recovering from her illness.*
>
> *She is recovering from her illness **slowly but surely**.*

As with other word classes, choose your adverbs carefully and wisely. Used sparingly, they can bring colour and variety to your writing.

TASK 1

Underline the adverbs in the following passage:

> *Tens of thousands of slightly damaged goods are being unnecessarily destroyed due to a defective screening system deployed at regional airports. Shipping agents collaboratively drafted an official statement to the Prime Minister in which their concerns were categorically stated. The Prime Minister has informally promised to address their issues soon.*

TASK 2

Incorporate the following adverbs into a paragraph of writing:

> *gingerly, surreptitiously, soon, yesterday, again,*
> *downstairs, suddenly, helplessly, sleepily, unnecessarily*

Make the setting your own home. Think carefully about your writing. Avoid using the words for the sake of using them and instead plan your work so that your ideas are linked, make sense and are well crafted.

_____

_____

_____

_____

_____

5. PRONOUNS

VOCABULARY DEVELOPMENT

Complete the grid. For each word, use a dictionary to identify the word class and meaning.

Word	Word class	Meaning
to urge		
offspring		
boundary		
wicket		
innings		
to applaud		
cholera		

IN THIS CHAPTER WE WILL COVER:

- Accurate use of pronouns/syntax.
- Effects of pronouns.
- Using pronouns for mood/atmosphere/setting.

Subject pronouns

Subject pronouns take the place of nouns (when used with verbs) to avoid repetition.

For example, you might say 'she' instead of 'Rose', 'it' instead of 'cat' and 'they' instead of 'the cricket players'.

	Singular pronouns	Plural pronouns
First person	I	We
Second person	You	You (plural)
Third person	He/she/it	They

Possessive pronouns

Possessive pronouns take the place of a possessive adjective and a noun:

- It's my pen = it's **mine**.
- It's your pen = it's **yours**.
- It's his/her/its pen = it's **his/hers/its**.

- It's our pen = it's **ours**.
- It's your pen = it's **yours**.
- It's their pen = it's **theirs**.

Often, people use 'me' when they should say 'I' and vice versa. An easy way of making sure you've chosen the right pronoun is to see if the sentence makes sense if you take away the additional person/people. In the examples below, 'Rose' is the additional person:

Rose and I are going to have a cup of coffee.

Correct: if we remove Rose from the sentence, we are left with: I [am] going to have a cup of coffee.

Rose and me are going to have a cup of coffee.

Incorrect: if we remove Rose from the sentence, we are left with: Me [is] going to have a cup of coffee.

I am going to have a cup of coffee (**correct**)

Me am going to have a cup of coffee (**incorrect**)

Notice also how the pronoun comes *after* the noun in the sentence: 'Rose and I are going to have a cup of coffee' not 'I and Rose are going to have a cup of coffee'.

Subject and object

In order to make the correct decision about which pronoun to use, you need to understand that nouns in a sentence are either the subject or object. Look at the following sentence:

The cat sat on the mat.

'Cat' and 'mat' are both nouns, but 'cat' is the subject because the verb 'sat' refers to the cat's actions, not the mat's. So, 'mat' is the object.

Whenever the pronoun is the **subject** of the sentence, use **I, you, he/she/it, we, your, their**. But whenever the pronoun is the **object** of the sentence, use **me, you, him/her/it, us, you, them**.

'The child followed him' is correct because the pronoun 'him' is the object of this sentence. It would not be correct to say 'The child followed he'.

'Aunt Joan spent her holiday with Mum and me' is correct because 'Mum and me' are the objects of the sentence. It would be incorrect to say 'Aunt Joan spent her holiday with Mum and I'.

'The cat sat on me' is correct because 'me' is the object of the sentence. It would be incorrect to say 'The cat sat on I'.

I think it is just Dad and me for supper tonight and he and I would be happy with a bowl

of soup.

In this instance, 'Dad and me' is correct because the subject of the first part of this compound sentence is 'I' so 'Dad and me' are the objects. Whereas, in the second part of the sentence, 'he [Dad] and I' are the subjects.

TASK 1

Underline the correct statements:

Me and my boyfriend are thinking of getting married.

My boyfriend and I are thinking of getting married.

Sarah, Jane, Matthew and I will all be there.

Sarah, Jane, Matthew and me will all be there.

It's time you and me had a chat.

It's time you and I had a chat.

She gave it to Gloria and I.

She gave it to Gloria and me.

The effects of pronouns

The effects of pronouns are various. Pronouns improve the flow and density of writing to avoid unnecessary repetition. And use of certain pronouns conveys information about characters and their relationships.

TASK 2A

Underline the **nouns** in the following paragraph:

Mr Michaels has a cat. Mr Michaels feeds his cat with meaty morsels. Mr Michaels

knows that his cat loves meaty morsels.

TASK 2B

Underline the **pronouns** in the following paragraph:

Mr Michaels has a cat. He feeds it meaty morsels. He knows that it loves them.

TASK 3

Read the following passage:

> 'Can I introduce you to my son?' said Mr Briggs, proudly producing the object of his affection, the 29-year-old Peter.
> 'Our son, darling,' corrected his wife from somewhere in the region of Mr Briggs' elbow.
> 'Oh sorry…yes. Our son, darling.'
> Mrs Briggs smiled but the colour in her face had risen and a shadow of resentment had appeared in her eyes.

Why is Mrs Briggs irritated? Give reasons for your answer.

_____

_____

_____

_____

_____

_____

_____

_____

TASK 4A

Read Roger McGough's poem *The Railings*.

You came to watch me playing cricket once.
Quite a few of the fathers did.
At ease, outside the pavilion
They would while away a Sunday afternoon.
Joke with the masters, urge on
their flannelled offspring. But not you.

Fielding deep near the boundary
I saw you through the railings.
You were embarrassed when I waved
and moved out of sight down the road.
When it was my turn to bowl though
I knew you'd still be watching.

Third ball, a wicket, and three more followed.
When we came in at the end of the innings
the other dads applauded and joined us for tea.
Of course, you had gone by then. Later,
you said you'd found yourself there by accident.
Just passing. Spotted me through the railings.

Speech-days • Prize-givings • School-plays
The Twentyfirst • The Wedding • The Christening
You would find yourself there by accident.
Just passing. Spotted me through the railings.

What does the poem reveal about the relationship between the speaker and his father?

_____

_____

_____

_____

TASK 4B

In what ways does the poet convey the speaker's attitude and feelings toward his father?

Pay attention to the diction (word classes) used and tone in your answer.

_____

_____

_____

_____

_____

_____

_____

TASK 4C

How is the title of the poem appropriate? How does it help you to understand and appreciate the message of the poem?

_____

_____

_____

_____

_____

_____

_____

TASK 4D

On the poem, underline how many times McGough uses the pronoun 'you' and write the number in the space below.

_____

Try experimenting with 'you'. Point at a friend or a member of your family and say 'you' three times in various tones of voice. What is the effect of this? How does it make the other person feel? Depending on your tone of voice, they might feel intimidated, accused or overwhelmed!

TASK 4E

Notice the use of plurals when describing the fathers and the cricket players and the use of the singular when describing the speaker's father. What is the effect of this?

_____

_____

_____

_____

TASK 4F

Form a circle with your family or friends around one person. Improvise a situation whereby the person in the middle of the group is isolated. Those in the circle can use 'we' and 'us' to refer to each other but 'you' or 'he/she' when referring to the person in the middle.

If someone were to witness this behaviour, they would feel uneasy. Why?

_____

_____

_____

_____

TASK 4G

For this creative writing activity, write a piece entitled 'You' to someone (fictitious) you feel has let you down. Adopt some of the techniques used by the speaker in McGough's poem:

- The pronoun 'you' used ubiquitously (lots of times).

- The phrases 'but not you', 'I knew you'd…', 'Of course…'

- A repeated mantra like 'Just passing. Spotted me through the railings'.

See below for an example of another pupil's work. This is particularly accomplished as Sophia's parents are very present and supportive. Yet, by adopting the techniques set out in the task, Sophia has conveyed a totally contrasting impression.

<u>You</u>

Every week you promised you'd come to my match, just like most other mums did. One time I was in the 'A' team against ****** yet again you were late; got there at half time, missing two of my goals.

Trying not to be seen, you would drive up near the netball court and stay in your car. When I took the side line ball, I caught your eye but you looked away. Every time I looked at you, you were on your phone. You said you were writing emails.

After that, the game was continued while I scored four more goals. After every goal, I looked at you but you weren't looking at me. Even though I knew you would be watching, obviously you'd be watching that's what I thought, that's what I told myself while other parents told their children about how amazing they were.

When we finished and we came in to pick player of the match, I was chosen. All my team mates and their mums came to congratulate me but when I looked over, when I thought you might be watching, you were gone.

Waiting in the line for match tea, Mrs. Newman was talking to me about the game, then she asked me if you came to watch. Of course I knew you were there but I told her you weren't because as usual you were writing emails.

I was the main lead in the school play, I was sports girly of the year I won pony extopians, I had my 18th birthday, I had my 21st birthday, you said you were busy, writing emails

Read your work out loud to someone. What is the tone of your writing? How has it been achieved?

TASK 5A

To begin exploring the role of pronouns in persuasive writing, underline all the pronouns in this charity appeal:

Yemen Crisis Appeal

Children in Yemen are struggling to survive bombs, terror and hunger. And right now they're dying from cholera. The disease is spreading fast. This deadly outbreak has already infected almost 400,000 children and adults.

A donation from you could help us save children's lives. Text ACT to 70008 to give £5. £40 of your money will buy a hygiene kit to protect children from this preventable disease.

TASK 5B

What is the persuasive effect of the different pronouns?

_____

_____

_____

_____

_____

_____

TASK 5C

Match each pronoun to an effect by drawing lines.

Pronoun	Effect
You ('A donation from you')	The use of the third-person plural pronoun makes it seem as if the number of children who need help is large.
They ('…they're dying…')	The use of the first-person plural pronoun makes the reader feel that by donating, she/he will be part of a team.
Us ('…could help us…')	The use of the second-person pronoun makes the reader feel personally addressed.

TASK 6A

As a revision exercise of your work on verbs, re-read the charity appeal and pick out examples of:

a) the imperative:

_____

b) the future:

_____

TASK 6B

Explain why using these tenses is persuasive in this context.

The imperative tense has the effect of being persuasive because _____

_____

_____

The future tense has the effect of being persuasive because _____

_____

_____

6. PREPOSITIONS

VOCABULARY DEVELOPMENT

Complete the grid. For each word, use a dictionary to identify the word class and meaning.

Word	Word class	Meaning
cabinet		
oblivious		
to throttle		

IN THIS CHAPTER WE WILL COVER:

- Prepositions.
- Identifying prepositions in context.
- Writing with prepositions.
- Sentences beginning with prepositional phrases.

PREPOSITIONS TELL US ABOUT 'POSITION' OR WHERE SOMETHING IS

Example of prepositions include: opposite, beneath, among, against, between, towards, aboard, across, within, along, over.

The function of prepositions is to improve the detail of our writing and to provide different focuses and perspectives.

TASK 1

Underline the prepositions in the following passage. The first one has been done for you.

<u>Beneath</u> her fingertips, the velvet sofa was soft. Subconsciously, she explored its covered studs and played with a loose thread dangling from the padded arm, but Taiya's attention was not focused on the sofa's pink material or on anything else in that well-known room: not the leather-backed books in the glass cabinet above the desk nor the black and white family photographs arranged along the shelves. She was oblivious, too, to the sounds of tennis and games of 'it' rising from the school grounds beneath the window.

Her head was drawn back, its angle titled stiffly toward the suited man in front of her, towering above her and shouting angry words. Showers of spit sprang from the angry, writhing mouth. His eyes bulged as if he were being throttled by unseen hands. Taiya seemed to be taking it all in but she felt curiously detached, as though she were an invisible observer. The words seemed to bounce around her and glance off her school uniform as though it were some sort of bulletproof vest. Taiya stifled a sudden and totally inappropriate urge to laugh.

TASK 2

Choose five prepositions to use in a paragraph of writing:

1. _____

2. _____

3. _____

4. _____

5. _____

Take time to plan your writing so that it tells a cohesive story and is not just a series of disconnected sentences containing prepositions. Begin one or more sentences with a prepositional phrase (e.g. 'Against the darkening sky', 'Inside my head', 'Behind the desk').

_____

_____

_____

_____

_____

_____

_____

_____

_____

_____

_____

7. CONJUNCTIONS

VOCABULARY DEVELOPMENT

Complete the grid. For each word, use a dictionary to identify the word class and meaning.

Word	Word class	Meaning
abundance		
sparse		
elongating		

IN THIS CHAPTER WE WILL COVER:

- Identifying conjunctions.
- Distinguishing between coordinating and subordinating conjunctions.
- Effects of conjunctions in context.
- Polysyndeton/asyndeton.

CONJUNCTIONS SERVE TO LINK IDEAS

The prefix con- derives from the Latin word *cum*, which means 'with'. Conjunctions improve the cohesion of our writing and allow us to build sentences.

Coordinating conjunctions

These include: and, but, until, or, yet, so.

> *I went to the post office several times. I met the postman. I asked him if he had a parcel for me. He said he hadn't. I wasn't surprised.*

> *I went to the post office several times* **until** *I met the postman* **and** *I asked him if he had a parcel for me,* **but** *he said he hadn't* **and** *I wasn't surprised.*

The second example is rather a clumsy (**compound**) sentence, but it makes the point that sentences can be linked with coordinating conjunctions.

Subordinating conjunctions

These are words and phrases such as: while, as soon as, although, before, even if, because, no matter how, whether, whenever, when, until, after, as if, if, provided, once, while, unless, as far as, now that, so that, though, since.

In Latin, *sub* means 'under', hence *sub*marine, *sub*way or *sub*ordinate (which means lower in status).

> *In the office, Mr Briggs is* **subordinate** *to Mrs Chakrabarti, who is the chairman of the company.*

That sentence contains a **subordinate clause**: 'who is the chairman of the company'. Although it contains a verb, it doesn't make sense on its own.

> **Whenever** *she sings in church, she gets a sore throat.*
> **Although** *Granny was nearly 92, she still had a childish sense of humour.*
> **Now that** *you have passed your driving test, you can collect the shopping.*

'Whenever she sings in church' doesn't make sense on its own. A main clause is required to make sense of it. The main clause, 'she gets a sore throat', *does* make sense on its own. The combination of a **main clause** and a **subordinate clause** creates a **complex sentence**.

TASK 1A

What is the effect of a list connected with a series of 'ands' (coordinating conjunctions)?

_____

_____

_____

_____

TASK 1B

Look back at the Jenny Joseph poem *Warning* on page 44. Count how many times Joseph uses the conjunction 'and':

_____

TASK 1C

What is the effect of this?

_____

_____

_____

_____

Polysyndeton and asyndeton

Items on a list are usually connected by a comma:

> *On our picnic, we ate barbecued chicken, salad, apples, crisps and chocolate brownies and drank home-made lemonade.*

If each item on this list is separated by the conjunction 'and', it reads:

> *On our picnic, we ate barbecued chicken **and** salad **and** apples **and** crisps **and** chocolate brownies **and** drank home-made lemonade.*

By using 'and' instead of commas, we increase the sense of abundance by physically elongating the list. The rhythm of the sentence is also slowed down, which allows the spotlight to linger on each item for longer. The sense of enthusiasm is increased.

You can try this at home. For example:

> **Parent**: *What have you done today?*
>
> **Child**: *I've tidied my room and washed my clothes and done my homework and vacuumed the stairs and written a thank-you letter to Auntie Jo.*

This technique is known as **polysyndeton**. The word 'polysyndeton' comes from Ancient Greek; it contains elements which mean 'many' and 'bound together'.

By contrast, **asyndeton** is a technique where conjunctions such as 'and' are left out. For example: 'I came. I saw. I conquered.' The effect is sparse and dramatic.

Conjunctions to change direction

Conjunctions such as 'but' and 'yet' serve to cause a change of direction:

> *I would love to come to dinner **but** I have work to do.*
>
> *She seems happy **yet** there is a sadness in her eyes.*

The words 'however' and 'although' also cause the direction to change:

> *I love chocolate **although** I know it's bad for my teeth.*
>
> ***However** hard Brian works, he struggles to keep on top of his workload.*

We rarely encounter words like 'however' and 'although' in poetry, but we often encounter 'but' and 'yet'. A possible reason is that 'but' and 'yet' are words of one syllable and a poet would not want to waste syllables unnecessarily. Look out for 'but' and 'yet' in the poems you study – they will always herald a transition or contrasting moment.

TASK 2

Look at Jenny Joseph's poem *Warning* again (page 44). Spot the first time she uses the conjunction 'but'. What happens to the focus of time when she does?

_____

_____

_____

_____

_____

_____

8. WRITING STRUCTURES

VOCABULARY DEVELOPMENT

Complete the grid. For each word, use a dictionary to identify the word class and meaning.

Word	Word class	Meaning
component		
cellar		
Dalmatian		
irony		
to herald		
rhetorical (question)		
to invoke		

IN THIS CHAPTER WE WILL COVER:

- The components of spoken and written language.
- The purpose and effects of different sentence structures.
- Punctuation for sentences.

WORDS
Help! Look!

PHRASES
Groups of words
which don't contain
a verb and which don't
make sense on their own:

*A loaf of fresh brown
bread; a violent outburst;
traces of peeling blue
paint; down by the water*

SUBORDINATE CLAUSES
Groups of words which contain a verb
but which don't make sense on their own:

*Provided you work, … ; Feeling unsteady, … ;
As soon as she woke up, … ; Now you've arrived, …*

MAIN CLAUSES/SIMPLE SENTENCES
Groups of words which contain a verb and
which do make sense on their own:

*She bought some grapes. Fatima is on top of
the world. That puppy is out of control.*

COMPOUND SENTENCES
One or more main clauses/simple sentences connected with conjunctions:

*She bought some grapes **and** ate them with chunks of
cheese. Fatima is on top of the world **but** Afra is down in the
dumps. That puppy is out of control **so** nobody likes it.*

COMPLEX SENTENCES
A combination of main and subordinate clauses:

*Provided you work, you will succeed. Feeling unsteady, she collapsed on to the sofa. As
soon as she woke up, she checked her mobile phone. Now you've arrived, we can start.*

Writing is made up of different components – words, phrases, subordinate clauses, main clauses, simple sentences, compound sentences, complex sentences and paragraphs.

The function of phrases within a sentence is to add extra detail:

> *She went down the stairs.*
> *She went down the stairs **to the cellar**.*

On their own, phrases can add a breathless, staccato quality.

No more time. Out of energy. Rising water levels. Lack of oxygen. Complete disaster.

TASK 1

Add phrases to the following simple sentences:

Mary ate her supper.

_____

_____

The Dalmatian bounded in.

_____

_____

The beech trees are shedding their leaves.

_____

_____

Prepositional phrases

These are very useful ways of varying how you start a sentence and they also serve to make your writing interesting by changing the focus. If they appear at the beginning of the sentence, they should be separated from the rest of the sentence by a comma. If they come at the end, there is no need for a comma.

> **Beneath her fingertips**, *the edge was jagged.*
> **At the end of the lane**, *the countryside was dense.*
> **Outside the window**, *she heard whispered voices.*
> *The edge was jagged* **beneath her fingertips**.
> *The countryside was dense* **at the end of the lane**.
> *She heard whispered voices* **outside the window**.

Other sorts of phrases

Noun phrases have a noun as their head. The noun is expanded to form a noun phrase:

The door (noun)
> = the green door with a brass knob and round spyhole (noun phrase).

Adjectival phrases have an adjective as their head. The adjective is expanded to form an adjectival phrase:

Dirty (adjective)
> = dirty with dead flies and thick dust (adjectival phrase).

Adverbial phrases contain adverbs, which describe verbs and can tell us more about the verb in terms of time, manner and place:

Soon (adverb expressing time)
> = she will arrive **soon, after six o'clock** (adverbial phrase expressing time).

Stiffly (adverb expressing manner)
> = he regarded the others **stiffly, a sneer on his face** (adverbial phrase expressing manner).

Across (adverb expressing place)
> = he looked **across the river, towards the church** (adverbial phrase expressing place).

Subordinate clauses

As we saw on page 70, subordinate clauses are groups of words which do contain a verb but don't make sense on their own.

One or more subordinate clauses work with a main clause to form a complex sentence. The prefix sub- means under or beneath and so the subordinate clause plays a supporting role to the main clause.

There are various ways of introducing a subordinate clause. The first is by using the subordinate conjunctions (while, as soon as, although, before, even if, because, no matter how, whether, whenever, when, until, after, as if, since, as far as, etc).

> *Whenever the sun comes out, my spirits lift.*
>
> *As far as I knew, she was still at home.*
>
> *Whatever she turns her hand to, she succeeds.*

Note that if the subordinate clause comes before the main clause, the two must be separated with a comma. If the subordinate clause comes afterwards, there is no need for a comma.

> *My spirits lift **whenever** the sun comes out.*
>
> *She was still at home **as far as** I knew.*
>
> *She succeeds **whatever** she turns her hand to.*

TASK 2

Add subordinate clauses to the following main clauses by using a subordinate conjunction. The first one has been done for you.

I didn't look up.

> *Although I wanted to, I didn't look up.*

We became great friends.

_____

I was secretly proud.

_____

I tore a page from his notebook.

_____

Present participle

Another technique for introducing the subordinate clause is the present participle. In these instances, we don't need to use an auxiliary verb with the present participle because the subordinate clause doesn't need to make sense on its own:

> ***Feeling*** *tired, she slumped into a chair.*
>
> *On* ***entering*** *the room, she burst into tears.*
>
> ***Running*** *down the hill, he broke his ankle.*

TASK 3

Add a subordinate clause to the following main clauses using a present participle. The first one has been done for you.

Tony swam up beside me.

> *Sensing I was in trouble, Tony swam up beside me.*

I was lost.

_____

We went fishing together.

_____

The car broke down.

_____

Relative pronoun

Another way to introduce the subordinate clause is the relative pronoun (who, whose, whom, which, that). This can also be called a 'relative clause'.

> *Mrs Briggs, **who** lives next door, is 100 years old.*
>
> *Mr Briggs, to **whom** we give our vegetables, is three years younger than his wife.*
>
> *The vegetables, **which** we give to Mr Briggs, are grown from seed.*
>
> *Mrs Briggs, **whose** husband enjoys fresh vegetables, is 100 years old.*

Notice that the subordinate clause interrupts the main clause and so is separated from the main clause by commas at either end.

TASK 4

Turn the following simple sentences/main clauses into complex sentences using a subordinate clause introduced by the relative pronoun that I have written in brackets. The first one has been done for you.

*Martha is two months older than me (**who**).*

> Martha, <u>who</u> is my best friend at school, is two months older than me.

*The weather is slowly improving (**which**).*

_____

*My sister has learnt to write her full name (**whose**).*

_____

*A local doctor came to visit (**in whom**)*

_____

Compound sentences

In science lessons, we learn that 'compounds' are a combination of elements. Similarly, compound sentences are a combination of one or more simple sentences linked by the coordinating conjunctions – for example, 'or', 'and' or 'but'.

*Meg went to the shops **and** bought some eggs.*

*Grandpa Joe is unable to walk **but** he can do pilates.*

*She can come to lunch **or** come to tea **but** she can't come to both.*

Complex sentences

As we have already seen, complex sentences comprise a main clause and one or more subordinate clauses. Unlike compound sentences where the different elements have equal status, complex sentences contain subordinate clauses which are less important and don't make sense on their own.

TASK 5

Identify the main clause and the subordinate clause in the following complex sentences.

When Meg went to the shops, she bought some eggs.

Although Grandpa Joe is unable to walk, he can do pilates.

She can't come to tea, if she comes to lunch.

TASK 6

Put commas in the correct places in the following complex sentences. Remember that the subordinate clause must be separated from the main clause by a comma if it appears at the **beginning** of the sentence. If it appears **after** the main clause, there is no need for a comma.

When I am older I will own my own business.

Bampton's river overflowed because of the heavy rain.

Feeling undermined Zach behaved very badly.

The jogger who was 50 years old barged into a woman on Wandsworth Bridge.

TASK 7

Decide whether the following are phrases or simple, compound or complex sentences and tick the correct column.

	Phrase	Simple	Compound	Complex
Carrying fishing nets and jam jars on a string, my brothers came to collect me.				
Everyone was excited by the news.				
Beyond any doubt				
My mother talked of getting a new car when my father went back to work.				
He held my arm and steered me towards the towpath.				
I was left alone in the garden.				
A few days later				
Mother, hearing the crash, ran up the stairs.				
I wrote a note to Jenny, which I got one of my brothers to deliver, that very night.				

Remember!

To create an exciting, staccato beat, writers tend to use phrases (e.g. 'out of breath', 'nowhere to go') and short, simple sentences (e.g. 'She collapsed', 'War was declared').

Compound and complex sentences are the structures chosen by writers to support extra detail; they create a more flowing rhythm (e.g. 'Beyond the meadow, the village, which was just a rising line of uneven rooftops and turrets, was just visible and, although she couldn't yet see the church, Emma could hear that someone was ringing the bells, loudly and clearly, in the middle of the week.').

9. CAPITAL LETTERS

VOCABULARY DEVELOPMENT

Complete the grid. For each word, use a dictionary to identify the word class and meaning.

Word	Word class	Meaning
twit		

The culture of texting and instant messaging has meant that inaccurate use of capital letters is becoming more common.

Capital letters (upper case) are always used for:

- The pronoun 'I'.
- The first word of a new sentence.
- The first word of a new sentence of speech.
- Proper nouns (people, places, nationalities and languages, known events).
- Names of days (Monday, Tuesday), months (January, February), public holidays (Easter, Christmas), but not seasons (autumn, winter, spring, summer).
- The key words in titles of books, poems, TV programmes, etc (*Cider with Rosie*, *The Tale of Tom Kitten*, *Child on Top of a Greenhouse*).

TASK 1

Correct and accurately rewrite the following:

i have a dog called 'dog'. he was named by my sister, sasha, when she was a toddler. a friend of ours called their dog 'someone' because they couldn't agree on a name. in the park they were heard shouting, 'someone, someone! come here at once.' caroline smith named her horse 'like a twit' so that as she entered the ring at the horse show the loudspeaker would announce, 'here is caroline smith riding like a twit.'

10. FULL STOPS, EXCLAMATION MARKS AND QUESTION MARKS

VOCABULARY DEVELOPMENT

Complete the grid. For each word, use a dictionary to identify the word class and meaning.

Word	Word class	Meaning
squire		
inn		
rigging	noun	
gushing	adjective	

Full stops

Full stops have various functions. Primarily, they **mark the end of sentences**. This may sound straightforward but, all too frequently, commas are used incorrectly instead. This is because there are often insecurities about the properties of a sentence. Where does a sentence begin and end? Therefore, where should a full stop go?

From the thorough work you have already completed on sentence structure, you will know that a sentence (whether it is simple, compound or complex) makes sense on its own, as it is a group of words containing a verb/verbs.

TASK 1

Here is an extract from *Treasure Island* by Robert Louis Stevenson (Usborne Classics Retold). Rewrite it, placing full stops and capital letters in the appropriate places.

> *the squire was staying at an inn by the docks as we walked over there, I saw the port's long quays and a great fleet of ships at anchor they were of all sizes and nations the sailors in one ship were singing on the decks in another, they were high in the rigging, hanging to threads that seemed no thicker than a spider's web*

_____

_____

_____

_____

_____

TASK 2

Find examples of the following structures in the passage from *Treasure Island*.

Phrases:

_____

_____

_____

Subordinate clauses:

_____

_____

Main clauses:

_____

_____

A subordinate clause introduced with the relative pronoun 'that':

_____

_____

Present participle accompanied by an auxiliary verb:

_____

_____

A present participle introducing a subordinate clause (therefore without an auxiliary verb):

_____

_____

A subordinating conjunction:

_____

_____

A complex sentence:

_____

_____

A compound sentence within a complex sentence:

_____

_____

By picking out these examples of different writing structures, we are learning to recognise them and identify them. This is a useful exercise but, more importantly perhaps, we are also learning to appreciate that fluent writing seems to combine these structures effortlessly to create well-crafted work that speaks to us clearly.

Another function of full stops is to **mark abbreviations**. For example, 6 a.m., 7 p.m., Wed., Dec., Prof. Janeena Williams, Rev. Andrew Capaldi.

A full stop is used to abbreviate Professor and Reverend, but it is not used to abbreviate Mister (Mr), Missus (Mrs), Doctor (Dr) or Saint (St). This is because the full stop is not needed if the abbreviation includes the first and last letters of the word being abbreviated.

Ellipsis

Sometimes a sentence concludes with three full stops (…). These three full stops are called an ellipsis. They either represent the fact that bits of text are missing or they indicate that something is implied from the end of the sentence:

> *'He is always late and you know what that means…'*

Ellipses (the plural of ellipsis) can suggest that someone's sentence has broken off because of some danger and so an ellipsis can create tension and mystery:

> *All we could make out was breathless gabbling but, distinctly, we heard her gasp,*
> *'I can't…'*

Exclamation marks

Exclamation marks are used instead of full stops to end sentences which are exclamations or imperatives.

> *Get out of here, now!*
> *Buy one today!*

After an exclamation mark, as after a full stop, the next word begins a new sentence and should have a capital letter.

Exclamation marks are a recognised feature of persuasive writing (such as advertisements or charity appeals) as they inject a sense of energy and urgency and call out to the reader, grabbing his/her attention.

> *Pick up the phone, now, please!*

Be sparing with exclamation marks. Used occasionally, they can convey drama, volume, humour, irony and excitement. Overuse can convey a gushing lack of control.

Question marks

Question marks are used instead of full stops at the end of sentences which are questions. A series of questions asked by a character in a story could convey uncertainty or fear:

> *Where am I? What's happening to me? Why are you here?*

After a question mark, as after a full stop or exclamation mark, the next word begins a new sentence and should have a capital letter.

Rhetorical questions (ones that are asked to make a point rather than to gain an answer) are a recognised feature of persuasive writing. They encourage the reader to engage with the topic:

> *Fancy a few days of warm sunshine and turquoise water?*
> *Can you stand by and watch these animals perish, needlessly?*

11. COMMAS, BRACKETS, DASHES AND HYPHENS

VOCABULARY DEVELOPMENT

Complete the grid. For each word, use a dictionary to identify the word class and meaning.

Word	Word class	Meaning
German shepherd		

Commas

Commas have various uses:

1. To separate items on a list.

    From the stationery shop, we bought a pen, some cartridges, HB pencils, coloured

    pencils, a ruler, a rubber, a sharpener and a red felt tip.

2. To separate subordinate clauses from main clauses, especially if they appear in front of the main clause, and to separate relative clauses.

    As soon as we woke up, we went running.
    Cycling across the field, she lost control of her bike.
    Mrs Brown, who lent us her car, has just become a grandmother.

3. To separate adverbs or adverbial phrases from the main body of the sentence.

    Suddenly, she burst into song.
    With all his might, he broke down the door.

4. In direct speech, to separate the 'he said' from the actual words spoken:

> *He said, 'There's no need to worry about it.'*
> *'There's no need to worry about it,' he said.*

Or, if the sentence of speech is interrupted:

> *'There's no need,' he said, sipping his tea, 'to worry about it.'*

The exception to this rule is if the speech itself is a question or exclamation:

> *'Stop him!' she shouted.*
> *'Did you see that?' he asked.*

5. To separate an aside:

> *She is not, of course, qualified.*
> *You are, by contrast, very hard-working.*

6. To separate a person's name from the rest of the sentence.

> *Thank you, Jaya, for bringing us home safely.*
> *Let me remind you, Wilder, that we wash our own plates.*
> *Sorry, Tom, for the misunderstanding.*

7. Commas can be used to introduce extra but non-essential information:

> *Our dog, the German shepherd, is having puppies.*
> *The local greengrocer, Mr Jones, is retiring.*

Brackets (also known as parentheses)

Brackets (..........) are used to separate an aside or an extra piece of information that is not essential to the sentence.

Mr Oluo (previously a teacher) is the local MP.

People often ask whether the punctuation should go inside or outside the brackets. There are various rules:

1. If an entire sentence is within brackets, the punctuation belonging to it stays with it inside the brackets. For instance:

Do read the whole letter. (You'll enjoy the third paragraph.)
Sadia and Bill set off at 6am. (They were still late!)
Bella didn't stay for tea. (I wonder why?)

2. If it is an aside within a complete sentence, there is no need for any punctuation within the brackets. For instance:

We will go on holiday (a working holiday) this Monday.
He left home at 3pm (having taken 30 minutes to say goodbye) and took our bicycle with him.

However, if the aside requires a question mark or an exclamation mark, then this should stay inside the brackets with the aside:

I need to finish my homework (or do I?) at 7pm.
Jemima made breakfast (if you can call it that!) every morning.

3. If the bracketed information comes at the end of the sentence, the punctuation for the sentence goes outside the bracket. For instance:

She did give me a birthday present (from her second-hand drawer).
We took the dogs for a walk (for four hours).

4. If the bracketed information is at the end of a clause that requires a comma, then the comma is included after the closing bracket. For instance:

Before the others arrived (after lunch), we spoke openly.
Whenever she goes to the gym (at the end of the road), she buys sweets on the way home.

Dashes

Dashes (–) can perform the same function as brackets but are used in a less formal way.

> *We've had a wonderful holiday – despite our earlier fears – sailing in the English Channel.*

They can also be used to add emphasis:

> *You may think she's dishonest – she's not.*
> *He might turn up – who knows?*

Hyphens

Hyphens (-) are used to join two or more words or parts of words together to make a compound word. For example:

> *up-to-date*
> *great-grandmother*
> *son-in-law*

The use of hyphens is constantly evolving. Email was once a hyphenated word, but it has become so widely used that it is now one word. Similarly, the word internet was once capitalised.

Hyphens can also eliminate ambiguity where there are two possible meanings. For example, 'twenty-odd people' means roughly twenty people, whereas 'twenty odd people' means twenty unusual people.

12. INDIRECT AND DIRECT SPEECH

VOCABULARY DEVELOPMENT

Complete the grid. For each word, use a dictionary to identify the word class and meaning.

Word	Word class	Meaning
bated (breath)		
eruption		

This table shows the difference between indirect and direct speech:

Indirect speech	Direct speech
She asked where the science labs could be found.	'Where can I find the science labs?' she asked.
He asked when lunch would begin.	He asked, 'When will lunch begin?'
They insisted that they hadn't moved anything.	'We haven't moved anything,' they insisted.

In our writing, direct speech enables us to develop our characters because how they say things – and what they do as they say them – can create more atmosphere. For example:

Indirect speech:

Mrs Fisher was cross and asked the class to explain why the whiteboard was swinging from its hinges.

Direct speech:

Mrs Fisher paced back and forth like a caged animal. The class waited with bated breath. She was about to erupt and the prospect of it was thrillingly dangerous. When the eruption came, it was no disappointment.
'How dare any of you touch the equipment in this classroom?' Mrs Fisher banged the desk and glared at the back row. 'I am sick and tired of your vandalism. Sick and tired of your deceit! If someone doesn't own up to this,' she gesticulated at the wrecked whiteboard with a sweep of her hand, 'you'll all be in trouble. The whole class will lose their breaks for a month.'

Rules for punctuating dialogue or direct speech

1. All words spoken are enclosed by inverted commas (speech marks), either double (") or single ('). Whichever you choose, be consistent.

> *'I am going to the shops,' announced Beverley.*

2. Speech marks must never close without some form of punctuation.

> *'I am in Belfast next week,' said Mikayla.*
> *Ari whispered, 'Keep your voices down. They're here.'*
> *'Watch out!' yelled Bella.*
> *'Where will you go?' sobbed Fred.*

3. 'He said' should be separated from the spoken words by a comma, whether it precedes the speech or comes afterwards.

> *He said, 'It's time to go home.'*
> *'It's time to go home,' he said.*

4. The first sentence of speech begins with a capital letter.

> *I whispered, 'Get the captain and squire to the cabin.'*

5. If the sentence of speech is interrupted, the continued speech does not need a capital letter.

> *'My lads, we've,' he faltered, 'we've reached our destination.'*

6. Each time a new speaker speaks, begin a new paragraph.

> *'Have any of you seen this place before?' he asked.*
> *'I have, Sir,' answered Silver.*
> *'The best anchorage appears to be off the North Bay,' replied Smollett.*

(The examples in 4, 5 and 6 are from *Treasure Island* by Robert Louis Stevenson, Usborne Classics Retold.)

Opposite are two pieces of creative writing by pupils who were asked to make use of the following lines of speech:

> *It made a noise.*
> *A frightening noise?*
> *No, no.*
> *A musical noise?*
> *A noise of scuffling?*
> *No, but a very loud noise like groaning.*
> *What did you do?*
> *I was coming to that.*

'IT MADE A NOISE!' BY CHARLOTTE

Jane Oakmore opened the door to a bedraggled Laura Sutton. Laura was wet through to the bone and her new coat was now dark and clinging to her like a coat of blue tack. Her blond hair was tangled and almost velcroed to her face. She was quite out of breath and only just managed to splutter out, '**It made a noise!**' pointing to the bush next to the phone box on the other side of the road.

Jane just stood there astonished. Her best friend, who she had seen walking out of her drive and to whom she had waved goodbye just a few hours earlier, was standing in front of her, rain dripping from her nose and shivering severely. Jane suddenly came to her senses and ushered Laura in. She sat her down by the fire and waited for Laura to warm up.

The wind outside whistled and banged against the window, the rain hammering constantly on the sky light above. There was no one to be seen and the road was empty of cars. Then, just as Laura was about to speak, Jane asked, '**A frightening noise?**'

'**No, no,**' Laura said rather quickly. She was beginning to fiddle with the button on her coat.

'**A musical noise? A noise of scuffling?**' Jane asked swiftly. She was becoming interested in the noise. Some excitement on Willow Lane for once!

Laura was still fiddling with the button on her coat, idly licking her finger and polishing the button until it reflected the dark, angry night outside. She then whispered, so that no one could hear, '**No, but a very loud noise, like groaning.**' She glanced out of the window at the phone box, trying not to look at Jane.

'**What did you do?**' Jane inquired.

'**I was coming to that,**' Laura said darkly.

'IT MADE A NOISE!' BY ALFRED

We ploughed on through the cellar towards the 1940s school rooms. The cellar seemed to regenerate as we went on. Who knew how Jake, Gus and I would escape from this cobwebby, spider-infested labyrinth. After a lot more shuffling and squeezing through nooks and crannies, we came upon a thin passageway. As I was the slimmest of us, I was the only one able to go on.

Cobwebs stuck to my face and hair and I was struggling for fresh air but the passageway finally led into what appeared to be cloakrooms in the WW2 school. A wooden door led out of it but when I placed my hand onto the doorknob to open it, the door shook vigorously. I jumped with surprise. I could not see what was happening because the only source of light was at the end of the passage I had come down.

As normal, in moments of tension, my fingers found the paperclip in my pocket; I started bending and twisting it to help me calm down and think.

Then, a very quiet banging noise came from behind the door. I backed away, my heart racing, digging the paperclip into my thumb's flesh. Somehow, I negotiated the passageway sideways like a crab for it was the only way to fit.

'**It made a noise,**' I said, my teeth clenched and dirty sweat dribbling into my mouth. The dirt made me choke and I cleared my dry throat. I heard muttering from the other two.

'**A frightening noise?**' said Jake with a tone of what people call sarcasm.

Gathering my wits, I thought about this question. '**No, no.**' This was a white lie because it was not a frightening noise but that does not mean I was not scared by it, but I couldn't show that to them. When I rejoined them at the end of the tunnel, they looked bored and were leaning against the wall. They looked impatient. I sat on a dusty barrel, panting.

Gus persisted with his questions. '**A musical noise?**' asked Gus.

'**A noise of scuffling?**' added Jake, a provocative smirk on his face. They had high expectations, I decided.

I stared at my paperclip, continuing to twist and bend it. I had to lie. '**No but a VERY loud noise, like groaning.**'

'**What did you do?**' Jake was either trying to wind me up or he was seriously intrigued. Suddenly I was angry. Angry at the way they continuously belittled me and angry with myself for playing into their hands. I hurled the paperclip towards him.

'**I was coming to that!**'

TASK 1

Use the following lines of dialogue/direct speech in a piece of creative writing. Use the opportunity to develop setting and characterisation:

I'm in Belfast next week.

Keep your voice down. They're here.

Watch out!

It's time.

13. APOSTROPHES

VOCABULARY DEVELOPMENT

Complete the grid. For each word, use a dictionary to identify the word class and meaning.

Word	Word class	Meaning
to omit		
to possess		
context		

Apostrophes for omission

Apostrophes for omission are those used to replace missing letters when two or more words are combined (or 'contracted') to form one word:

- I have = I've
- You cannot = you can't
- It is = it's
- They are = they're
- We would = we'd
- I am = I'm

Contractions are one of the features of informal writing. Non-contractions are one of the features of formal writing.

Features of informal writing	Features of formal writing
Contractions: I'm, you're, there's	Non-contractions: I am, you are, there is
Active voice: I can see Windsor Castle; She drives the car	Passive voice: Windsor Castle can be seen; The car is driven by her
Colloquial (informal) language: Kids can play on the climbing frames; Mums and dads are welcome	Formal language: Children may play on the apparatus; Parents are welcomed

Apostrophes for possession

Apostrophes for possession are those used to demonstrate ownership. The apostrophe goes after the 'possessor':

The boys possess cricket bats = the boys' cricket bats.

The cricket bats belong to the **boys** so the apostrophe goes after the word '**boys**'.

The boy possesses a cricket bat = the boy's cricket bat.

The cricket bat belongs to the **boy** so the apostrophe goes after the word '**boy**'.

The ladies possess a changing room = the ladies' changing room.

The changing room belongs to the **ladies** so the apostrophe goes after the word '**ladies**'.

The woman possesses a suitcase = the woman's suitcase.

The suitcase belongs to the **woman** so the apostrophe goes after the word '**woman**'.

TASK 1

Convert the following statements into phrases which correctly convey possession by using an apostrophe. The first one has been done for you.

Statement	Phrase
Robyn possesses a dog	*Robyn's dog*
The geese possess feathers	
The child possesses a shoe	
The children possess a classroom	
The mouse possesses some cheese	
The girls possess some basketballs	

Potential difficulties

Difficulties arise from confusion between the possessive apostrophe and the possessive adjective/pronoun. People remember that 'its' and 'their(s)' have something to do with possession, so they must need an apostrophe, right?

But remember, 'its' and 'their(s)' do not need an apostrophe as they are not contractions and they are already possessive pronouns. They no more need an apostrophe than other possessive pronouns such as my/mine.

TASK 2

Rewrite the following sentences correctly:

Whos the partys candidate for vice president this year?

_____

_____

The horses right foreleg was caught by the fences wire.

_____

_____

_____

Our neighbours car -a Nissan – has a scratch on its bonnet.

_____

_____

She did not hear her childrens cries.

_____

_____

The dogs bark was worse than its bite.

_____

_____

The animals food was given to them every evening at 6.

_____

_____

14. COLONS AND SEMICOLONS

VOCABULARY DEVELOPMENT

Complete the grid. For each word, use a dictionary to identify the word class and meaning.

Word	Word class	Meaning
provocative		
benevolence		
conspicuous		
gratis	adverb	
filberts		
to entreat		
to beseech		

Colons

Colons (:) are used to introduce a list or a quotation.

There are two options: face up to your difficulties or change schools.
For your holiday, you must remember to take: swimming costume, goggles, reading books and sun cream.
The poet uses alliteration in line 3: 'blown bubbles of blue'.

Colons can also be used to link two main clauses when the second qualifies the first.

She deserved to be sacked: she was very provocative.

Semicolons

Semicolons (;) are used to separate items on a list which are already subdivided by commas.

For your holiday, you must remember to take: the black, backless swimming costume; goggles, snorkel and mask; sun cream, insect repellent and shampoo; and reading books.

TASK 1

Rewrite the following list from *A Christmas Carol* by Charles Dickens, placing commas and semicolons as appropriate.

There were pears and apples clustered high in blooming pyramids there were bunches of grapes made in the shopkeepers' benevolence to dangle from conspicuous hooks that people's mouths might water gratis as they passed there were piles of filberts mossy and brown recalling in their fragrance ancient walks among the woods and pleasant shufflings ankle deep through withered leaves there were Norfolk Biffins squab and swarthy setting off the yellow of the oranges and lemons and in the great compactness of their juicy persons urgently entreating and beseeching to be carried home in paper bags and eaten after dinner.

TASK 2

Dickens creates a vivid sense of abundance in the extract. What different techniques (find three, at least) has he used to achieve this? Support your answer with quotations from the text. Explain each point. *(6 marks)*

_____

_____

_____

_____

_____

_____

_____

_____

_____

_____

_____

Semicolons can also be used to separate two main clauses (which might otherwise be separated by a conjunction to form a compound sentence). The effect not only condenses writing but can also increase its impact.

> She had good A level grades and went to Oxford = She had good A level grades; she went to Oxford.
> The dog was unpredictable and bit children = The dog was unpredictable; it bit children.
> The sky was clear but it was unbearably humid = The sky was clear; it was unbearably humid.

After a semicolon used as above, a capital letter is not needed.

TASK 3

Rewrite the following extract from the Victorian novel *North and South* by Elizabeth Gaskell, applying capital letters, semicolons and other punctuation where appropriate.

> they did not speak their hearts were too full another moment and the train would be
> here a minute more and he would be gone

_____

_____

_____

_____

_____

15. FURTHER IDEAS FOR CREATIVITY, CRAFTSMANSHIP AND ANALYSIS

VOCABULARY DEVELOPMENT

Complete the grid. For each word, use a dictionary to identify the word class and meaning.

Word	Word class	Meaning
chronology		
subtle		
subtleties		
to dispel		
derogatory		
pejorative		
to depict		
deterioration		
to evoke		
capacity		
connotation		
dilapidation		
emaciated		
to juxtapose		
adjacent		
to replicate		
predatory		
introspection		
irresistible		
to endorse		
detrimental		
covetous		

Word	Word class	Meaning
intriguing		
to elicit		
habitually		
to advocate		
indigenous		

Enthusiasm is infectious. Pupils like to witness their mentors reading and writing alongside them or sharing their thoughts and systems with them. Poems, song lyrics and extracts of great writing from the present and past are excellent starting points for planning and craftsmanship. This chapter presents 10 resources to help mentors develop their pupils' skills of creativity, craftsmanship and analysis.

The resources

THE CHRONOLOGY OF ENGLISH LITERATURE

To develop curiosity and independent study, schools can create a frieze which provides a chronology of English literature and key historical events. Finding an author or poet on the frieze is a good starting point for independent research before introducing a new writer to pupils. Parents at home can do something similar. Knowing which king or queen was on the throne at different times and having some context within which to study has a grounding effect on everyone.

It's just as straightforward to create a document as an easy form of reference.

A Chronology of English Literature

Dates	Period and Context	Features	Key works (seminal in bold)
700 800 900	**Old English – 'Oral Tradition'** • Anglo-Saxons have invaded; language is Germanic (Angles, Saxons and Jutes) and later influenced by Old Norse via Viking invasions • Several dialects, with West Saxon dominant due to King Alfred. Latin is still the language of writing and learning	• Fixed poetic form – no rhyme; three-fold alliteration/stress • Kennings eg 'night stalker' (Grendel), 'whale road' (sea) • Heroic/religious content. Oral tradition prevails (designed to be spoken/heard)	*Beowulf* – epic poem *Hymn to Creation* (Caedmon) *Dream of the Road* – told from the point of view of the crucifix
1000 1100 1200 1300 1400	**Middle English – 'English Emerges'** • Old English merges with Norman French after Norman Conquest in 1066 • By 14th C, London is seat of government and trade • Printing press invented, revolutionises literacy/communications (Gutenberg 1440); brought to England by Caxton, 1474 • Chaucer's choice to write in London dialect begins the acceptance of English as a 'literary' language	• Rhyme royal (deco-syllabic) esp in *Troilus and Criseyde* • Most of *Canterbury Tales* is rhyming couplets • Starts to be recognisable to the modern ear as English • English gains words from French with upper class connotations, as they are the ruling class, while English words remain for farming/labouring words (eg 'pork' vs 'pig')	*Sir Gawain and the Green Knight* (c. 1340) – the story of Arthurian legend (a romance brought from France) *Pearl* – moving poem about the loss of a child – perhaps same anonymous author as Gawain *Canterbury Tales* (c. 1390) (Geoffrey Chaucer) – a group of pilgrims on their way to Canterbury tell each other tales, some bawdy
1500	**Early Modern / Renaissance – 'Explosion of Creativity'** • Break with Rome/Catholicism drives new drama/theatre • Rediscovery of classical Greek/Roman literature • Italian influence • Public theatre hugely popular for all strata of society from peasants to royalty • Writers tried to curry royal favour with their works, e.g. *Macbeth* appealed to King James's fascination with witches; Thomas More was a close confidant of Henry VIII but stuck to Catholic principles and lost his head for it! • Strict gender expectations; women not allowed to act	• Formal styles of poetry eg sonnets (14-line poems with particular format) • Plays and theatre make use of blank verse, iambic pentameter, heroic couplets, for different effects • Play scripts were often only given to actors in parts, the whole script existing for the prompter from the start; actors had parts only. Published texts derived from several sources becoming 'complete' plays after author's death (as with Shakespeare) • Creativity in all aspects of language – new words invented, word classes changing (verbification), influence of trade with newly emerging Empire • Use of 'elevated' (fancy) language to imitate Latin	*Utopia* (Thomas More 1478-1535) – significant because the 'ideal' society he depicted became a model for future writers eg Swift, William Morris, H G Wells, Orwell, Huxley, and even modern works like *Hunger Games* **Various comedies (eg *Merry Wives of Windsor*), tragedies (eg *Hamlet, Romeo & Juliet*), histories (eg *Henry V*), sonnets (Shakespeare 1564-1616)** Elizabethan works – *Dr Faustus* (Christopher Marlowe) about making a pact with the devil; Jacobean works – *Duchess of Malfi* (John Webster); *The Changeling* (Thomas Middleton)
1600	**17th Century – 'Emerging Anxieties'** • A period of unprecedented turbulence and change: Gunpowder plot, Civil War, Commonwealth, Restoration • No public theatre performances during the commonwealth and when they resumed during Restoration, Shakespeare seemed 'remote' and Chaucer needed to be translated	• Drama declines after 1620s and print is now the norm • Metaphysical poets explore philosophical ideas, often with bizarre imagery, difficult verse forms and ideas borrowed from science and theology.	*Pilgrim's Progress* (John Bunyan 1678) – about a spiritual, religious journey and the perils of life *Oroonoko* (Aphra Behn 1688) – female playwright **Metaphysical poets – John Donne, Andrew Marvell**

2 POINTS AND EFFECTS

Techniques for creating a vivid picture or tension, or for persuading readers to think in certain ways, appear time and again in writing.

The Points and Effects resource has helped generations of learners to look out for some of these techniques or 'points', and to understand the ways in which different techniques work to create different effects. Familiarity with the resource helps pupils to appreciate the subtleties of language and structure and how meanings are conveyed.

The resource is designed to develop awareness. With guidance, it should dispel the temptation to learn techniques and their effects 'parrot-fashion' and be a revision guide for remembering techniques and their possible effects. It helps pupils not only to **identify techniques** and their **effects** but also to **explain** them.

Literature referred to:

Hunger by Laurence Binyon

Dulce et Decorum Est by Wilfred Owen

Wind by Ted Hughes

The Ice Cart by Wilfred Gibson

Autobiographical Note by Vernon Scannell

Above Penmaenmawr by Tony Connor

The Listeners by Walter de la Mare

Anthem for Doomed Youth by Wilfred Owen

The Hero by Siegfried Sassoon

April Rise by Laurie Lee

Badger by John Tripp

The Tyger by William Blake

The Eagle by Alfred, Lord Tennyson

A Cat by Edward Thomas

Blackberry-Picking by Seamus Heaney

Extract from *Journey's End* by R. C. Sherriff

'Fork handles' sketch by the Two Ronnies

Bird in the Classroom by Colin Thiele

Extract from *My Left Foot* by Christy Brown

It Ain't What You Do, It's What It Does to You by Simon Armitage

Extract from *The Crossing* by Kathy Watson

How does a writer/poet create a vivid picture (prose and poetry)?

Vivid pictures in both prose and poetry are created using the following descriptive 'points' or 'techniques':

 A IMAGERY

 B PRECISE DICTION

 C SENSES

 D LISTS

 E RHYTHM AND RHYME

 IMAGERY

When we look in the mirror, we receive an image of ourselves. Photographs capture these images so that they are frozen in time. Paintings can be close reproductions of reality, although they can often be distorted by the artist's own feelings and perceptions of their subject.

Writers create images by using words and phrases. A writer's use of similes and metaphors – in which one object or idea is compared to something else – creates images which help to bring descriptions into sharper focus.

Similes are introduced with the words 'as' or 'like', whereas a **metaphor** goes one step further and the object is described in terms of its comparison, without the need for 'as' or 'like'. **Personification** is a form of metaphor and is the technique used by writers to imbue inanimate objects with living characteristics. For example, a tree's branches might be referred to as its limbs and its twigs as bony fingers. Personification has the effect of giving inanimate objects a sense of life or a will of their own, or it can make them seem full of unpredictable energy.

When explaining the effect of a simile or metaphor, it is insufficient to say that 'it creates a clear picture'. You must work hard to explain how and why a 'clear picture' is being created in

terms of, for instance, its shape, scale, texture, colour, personality, etc. For example:

> 'bent double like old beggars under sacks' (simile from *Dulce et Decorum Est* by Wilfred Owen)

This simile is effective because 'old beggars' conjures up a derogatory image of elderly, struggling tramps; it is a cruel image depicting the suffering and deterioration of young men fighting on the front line in World War I.

> *rainwater boiled in puddles*
> (metaphor)

The verb 'boiled' conveys a picture of the rain falling so heavily and fiercely that the water in the puddles is bubbling like boiling water in a pan.

> 'Winds stampeding the fields under the window' (personification from *Wind* by Ted Hughes)

The verb 'stampeding' suggests that the wind is like an out-of-control beast, evoking its unpredictable strength and capacity for danger.

B PRECISE DICTION

Writers create clearer, more sharply focused pictures by choosing specific words, carefully, from the basic word-bank of nouns, verbs, adjectives and adverbs.

Nouns

Precise nouns: farmer/soldier/postman instead of just 'man' create a clearer picture.

A group of nouns: field/meadow/hedgerows/tractor contribute to a strong sense of setting.

Adjectives

Adjectives are words which describe nouns.

> 'o'er sapphire berg and emerald floe,
> beneath the still, cold ruby glow'
> (from *The Ice Cart* by Wilfred Gibson)

These 'jewel' adjectives create a bright, exotic picture.

> 'broken', 'overgrown', 'unroofed'
> (from *Above Penmaenmawr*
> by Tony Connor)

These adjectives contribute to a picture of dilapidation.

Emotive adjectives

Emotive adjectives are adjectives which work on our emotions.

> *huddled, exhausted, emaciated*

These words make us feel sorry and sympathetic.

> *refreshing, invigorating*

These make us feel exhilarated.

Verbs

Identify, gather and look at the verbs used. Is there a pattern?

> *Huddled, staggered*

These create a sense of waning energy.

> *Glared, laboured*

These create a sense of intensity.

Adverbs

Adverbs are words which describe verbs; they tell us more about how something has moved and create further detail and atmosphere.

> ***Suddenly***, *Gwen burst into tears…*
> ***Gingerly***, *she teased apart the tissue paper…*

C SENSES

Writers make reference to the five senses (sight, hearing, touch, taste, smell) to inject a sense of life into their writing. Sometimes they make direct reference to senses: *I could hear nothing but the sound of the clock ticking, a log hissing in the grate and, somewhere outside, a dog barking.*

At other times they may use more discreet techniques such as onomatopoeia (of which sibilance, plosives, fricatives, etc. are examples), alliteration and assonance.

Onomatopoeia and alliteration

Onomatopoeia means words which have a phonic quality or sound as they are. Alliteration means juxtaposed words which begin with the same sound.

Alliteration can be used to emphasise words' onomatopoeic qualities:

> *'forest's ferny floor'*
>
> (from *The Listeners* by Walter de la Mare)

The repetition of 'f' has a soft, padded effect (fricatives).

> *'silence surged softly'*
>
> (from *The Listeners* by Walter de la Mare)

The hissing sound (sibilance) created by the 's' repetition evokes the whispery sounds of silence.

> *'blown to bits'*
>
> (from *The Hero* by Siegfried Sassoon)
>
> *'blown bubble of blue'*
>
> (from *April Rise* by Laurie Lee)
>
> *'red slippery pulp'*
>
> (from *Badger* by John Tripp)

'P' and 'b' are rounded, rubbery sounds (plosives).

> *'cattles' rapid rattle'* (from *Anthem for Doomed Youth* by Wilfred Owen)

The 'r' alliteration and 't' repetition sound like machine-gun fire.

> *'he clasps the crag with crooked hands'*
>
> (from *The Eagle* by Alfred, Lord Tennyson)

These 'ck' sounds create a hard, brittle effect.

> *'...locked her out of doors at bedtime*
>
> *and had her kittens duly drowned'*
>
> (from *A Cat* by Edward Thomas)

Note the use and repetition of hard 'd' sounds to create a forbidding sense of finality.

Assonance

Assonance refers to sounds within syllables that are replicated by nearby words (s**o**nnet/p**o**rridge) or echoed by nearby words (k**ill**ed/c**o**ld/c**ull**ed), also known as 'half-rhyme'.

> *'...a glossy purple **clot**'*
>
> *'...red, green, hard as a **knot**'*
>
> (from *Blackberry-Picking* by Seamus Heaney)

The short-syllabled assonance of 'clot' and 'knot' evokes the small, round shape of blackberries.

> *'jam-pots'/'boots'*
>
> *'potato-drills'/'full'*
>
> *'byre'/'fur'*
>
> (from *Blackberry-Picking* by Seamus Heaney)

These half-rhymes create aural links that connect ideas less obviously.

D LISTS

Writers can create a clearer picture through the use of lists because they increase detail.

Lists separated by commas

Increase detail, introduce a staccato rhythm and can simply emphasise the scale of something.

Lists separated by the conjunction 'and' (polysyndeton)

Allow the spotlight to fall on each item on a list, thereby adding extra emphasis to each item.

> *'Stay and see it out with decent men like*
> *Osborne **and** Raleigh **and** Trotter'*
> (from *Journey's End* by R. C. Sherriff)

No commas in a list (asyndeton)

Creates a staccato rhythm adding dramatic impact to each element.

> *'He came. He saw. He conquered.'*

E RHYTHM AND RHYME

Rhythm and rhyme are important elements of poetry. (Different sentence types can also influence the rhythm of prose.) Rhythm and rhyme contribute to the meaning of poems in various ways, creating different but equally vivid pictures.

> *'Tyger! Tyger! Burning bright*
> *In the forests of the night'*
> (from *The Tyger* by William Blake)

Here, the rhythm is regular, the rhyme repetitive (rhyming couplets) and it follows a consistent pattern throughout to convey the tiger's predatory strength and energy.

> *'Winds stampeding the fields under*
> *the window*
> *Floundering black astride and blinding wet'*
> (from *Wind* by Ted Hughes)

Throughout Hughes' poem there is no rhyme scheme or rhythm. Sentences cross stanzas (enjambment) to evoke the fact that this wind is so strong it cannot be contained within a tidy structure; it is out of control.

2

How do writers create feelings of tension and excitement or build suspense?

A writer begins with a blank page, but various techniques can cause readers to feel tense and excited. The following techniques are often to be found in tense writing.

● SHORT SENTENCES/ EXCLAMATIONS

These introduce a staccato rhythm which speeds up the action, a little like the sound heard in the film *Jaws* (*der-d, der-d, der-d*) when the man-eating shark was lurking.

● INTERMITTENT/OBSCURED LIGHTING

Candlelight/firelight/headlights/lightning/ torchlight/fog have the effect of creating shadows in which dangers may lurk.

● 'DISMEMBERMENT'

Murmured voices were heard from

the cellar.

Soft footsteps crunched through

the gravel.

The gloved hand closed softly

around my...

'Dismemberment' withholds the full identity of the person/people, increasing mystery. As 'dismemberment' is an invented term for this technique, we put it in inverted commas and explain it thoroughly.

● ANY TECHNIQUE WHICH WITHHOLDS INFORMATION OR MAKES TIME PASS SLOWLY

For example: a close introspection of inner thoughts, a focus on senses, an ellipsis, a countdown ('Five minutes had passed...')

These techniques have the effect of holding up the action, thereby creating suspense.

● ADVERBS

Suddenly..., Gingerly..., Furtively...

These adverbs inject varied pace and energy.

● A FOCUS ON A PHYSICAL REACTION TO EMOTION

Clammy hands, beating heart, sweating, for example. Readers may share these physical sensations, which are the body's natural responses to tension, and so a dramatic atmosphere is created.

● USE OF PUNCTUATION

Ellipses (...) create a mysterious sense of space or suspense.

Exclamation marks (Help! Stop right there!) signify drama!

Question marks (Where am I? Who is she? What's happening?) create a sense of uncertainty or doubt.

How does a writer create humour?

Writers can create humour in the following ways:

 EXAGGERATION OR HYPERBOLE

This can be exaggerated behaviour or exaggerated depictions of characters (caricature or stereotypes) to form amusing images.

 MISUNDERSTANDING

For example, the Two Ronnies sketch in the hardware store, where 'fork handles' is misinterpreted as 'four candles' because of the accent of one of the Ronnies. Once the sketch has set us up to expect misunderstandings, we anticipate others (saw tips/sore tips; hoes/hose/'o's) which becomes funny.

 SLAPSTICK

People falling over or playing practical jokes reminiscent of traditional clowns.

 SARCASM AND IRONY

Used to say the opposite of what is actually meant and intended to make the subject look foolish. For example: a pupil dressed top to toe in silver and carrying an axe to play the part of the Tin Man in *The Wizard of Oz* is asked, 'What part are you playing?'

 RHYTHM AND RHYME

Rhythm and rhyme can draw attention to particular word endings or create a non-serious, light-hearted tone.

Persuasive writing

Writing has many practical purposes: to inform, instruct, discuss, argue, describe and **persuade**.

Campaign leaflets, prospectuses, advertisements and political propaganda are designed to persuade people to do things, such as donate money to good causes, choose between schools, buy goods or vote differently.

Various techniques of language and structure are specifically employed by writers to work on readers in various ways.

Here are some of the persuasive features of language.

PUNS/IRONY/EXCLAMATION MARKS

For humour and to engage interest.

USE OF PERSONAL PRONOUN 'YOU'

Please, if you can, send a donation today.

Makes the reader feel personally addressed/ directly engaged.

USE OF RHETORICAL QUESTIONS

Feeling tired? Need a break?

Engages the reader, draws him/her into the text to find out answers to questions and makes the reader feel directly involved.

USE OF PERSONAL PRONOUNS 'WE' AND 'OUR' (FIRST-PERSON PLURAL)

We urgently need your help to provide emergency shelter.

Makes the reader feel part of a team/included; works on the irresistibility of the 'let's' factor.

REPETITION

Creates emphasis. (Alliteration 'repeats' the sounds at the beginning of juxtaposed words and also has the effect of creating emphasis or the feeling of relentlessness.)

USE OF FACTS AND FIGURES

23,000 deaths a year are linked to alcohol; In the worst floods to hit Somalia in over 30 years…

Adds the weight of truth, particularly when juxtaposed with (put alongside) opinion.

USE OF THE WORDS 'ONLY' AND 'JUST'

*It costs **just** £5 to buy and transport enough high-energy food to sustain one child for a month.*

This makes the effort sound minimal/easy.

USE OF QUOTATIONS

To endorse/support the view and make the reader feel part of a tried and tested team. If it's used by someone famous/successful, it must be OK.

USE OF IMPERATIVE TENSE

Buy one today!
Act now!

Injects a sense of urgency.

USE OF FUTURE TENSE

*With your help, **we'll** be able to…*
***You'll** need to buy a ticket today…*

Makes the reader feel already partially persuaded.

ANECDOTES

A story which illustrates a point, perhaps with dialogue/humour.

Anecdotes provide variety, create an animated diversion, paint a clearer picture and engage the reader.

COUNTER-ARGUMENT

*Your ideas are sound **but** changes still need to be made.*
*Fast food is convenient if used sparingly **but**, as it contains excessive amounts of salt and sugar, can be detrimental to health long-term.*
*Running is beneficial for developing aerobic fitness **although** it can put an unnecessary strain on joints.*

Gives an impression of a fair, balanced view, which is more persuasive.

LIST OF THREE

With your help, we can buy blankets, shelter and food packs.

Allows persuasive detail to be included.

EMOTIVE LANGUAGE

*Crops and stores of food have been **decimated** – a **malnourished** child is especially **vulnerable**…*

Works on readers' emotions in various ways. A writer may use words which sound appealing. Stirs feelings and evokes sympathy.

2

Persuasive features of form/structure/layout

BOXED INFORMATION, PARAGRAPHS, COLUMNS, SHORT PARAGRAPHS

All convey an impression of being organised and add variety.

BULLET POINTS, NUMBERED POINTS

Make information more accessible.

ITALICS, BOLD, DIFFERENT FONT SIZES/COLOURS

Allow different information to be emphasised.

BOLD HEADINGS

Catch the reader's attention; engage their interest.

EMOTIVE PICTURES

These stir feelings. For example, pictures of vulnerable members of society (animals, elderly people, little children) might make readers feel angry, indignant, sympathetic, etc. Pictures of exotic locations, delicious-looking food, holiday resorts and people laughing and smiling might make readers feel enthusiastic/covetous.

General advice on questioning or interpreting different comprehension questions

A: What is your attitude to…?
B: Describe the relationship between…?
C: How effective is the beginning or ending of…?
D: What is the significance of…?
E: How has humour been created in…?

F: Comment on the style of…
G: What is your response to…?
H: What are your impressions of…?
I: How has uncertainty/doubt been created in…?
J: How does the writer make you sympathise with…?

A ATTITUDE TO:

This is asking candidates to find adjectives which describe their attitude, supported by techniques which convey the attitude. Someone might have a **conscientious** attitude, a **lazy** attitude, an **indifferent** attitude, a **passionate** attitude, etc. Try to avoid saying 'a bad/good attitude' or 'a positive/negative attitude' – be specific.

B RELATIONSHIP BETWEEN:

So often, when asked to describe the relationship between people, candidates start to describe the people. Actually, pupils are being asked what the relationship is **between** two people. One might be subservient to the other, one might be domineering. A relationship could be described as stormy, peaceful, irascible, lacking respect and trust, etc.

C BEGINNINGS/ENDINGS:

Sometimes, candidates are asked to comment on the 'beginning' of a piece of writing and whether it is considered to be 'effective'. An effective beginning to a story or poem or play is one which immediately attracts attention and engages us. A writer can achieve this in a number of ways, such as beginning with something very dramatic or unusual, beginning with dialogue or in the middle of something intriguing, or describing a situation that poses questions to which we can only discover answers by reading on.

When asked to comment on the 'ending' of a poem or a piece of writing, think about how it ties in with what the material is about or what is written in the title. The poem *Hunger* by Laurence Binyon diminishes in length of stanza until it is one word. This is appropriate because hunger also reduces the flesh on a body.

In the poem *Bird in the Classroom* by Colin Thiele, the monotony of the teacher's voice is broken by the sudden arrival of a bird in the classroom; the ending suggests that the episode has taught the children to reflect on the wisdom of nature v mankind. In other words, a journey has occurred and with it a transition: the children began the lesson thinking they would learn nothing, but after the 'drama' of the bird, they have been prompted to think more deeply about life and its issues.

D THE SIGNIFICANCE OF:

This means: why is x, y or z important? In an extract from *My Left Foot* by Christy Brown, 'The Letter "A"', which relates the moment when Christy, who has cerebral palsy, picks up a piece of chalk and writes a letter for the first time, the moment is important or significant because Christy Brown went on to be a writer. This moment is the first step on that journey.

For the poem *It Ain't What You Do, It's What It Does to You* by Simon Armitage, candidates were asked to comment on the significance of this title. The answer is that it is significant because the poem is about different people being profoundly affected by different experiences: one person is affected by exhilarating leaps from planes, the other from skimming stones across a local pond in the North of England. Other episodes like this are contrasted throughout the poem. The fact that the title is written in non-standard English tells us there are non-standard ways of being profoundly affected in life.

E HUMOUR:

Sometimes candidates are asked to comment on how something is light-hearted or comical. Or they may be asked to pick up on the fact that the mood is humorous. Look for examples of slapstick humour (people falling about, being turned upside down, being made to look foolish in a light-hearted way). Look for examples of exaggeration: perhaps the characters have been turned into caricatures, or perhaps superlatives or hyperbole (another word for exaggeration) have been used. Perhaps there has been some misunderstanding which has caused amusement.

F STYLE:

This will refer to the types of sentences or punctuation used and their effects. It may refer to the use of non-standard English or to the rhythm or rhyme within poetry.

G RESPONSE TO:

This question invites candidates to provide an opinion: what **you** think and **why** you think it.

In the poem *Badger* by John Tripp, the last line is: 'Before a smallholder blew his head off.' Pupils are asked how they respond to the sudden, brutal death of the badger. The answer might be that it shocked them because it was so abrupt, and because it presented a contrast to the way the writer had invited us to dislike the

badger up until that moment. Now we feel sorry for the badger. The last line made us realise how cruel the laws of nature are.

H IMPRESSIONS OF:

Once again, candidates are being asked to find adjectives which describe their thoughts or impressions about something or someone:

> I thought them to be **unkind** or
>
> **cruel** because…
>
> I felt they were **distant** and **remote**
>
> because…

I UNCERTAINTY/DOUBT:

To create uncertainty, maybe the writer has used a series of questions. Maybe the writer has used imprecise adjectives such as 'hazy' or words such as 'perhaps' or 'possibly'. Maybe indistinct verbs have been used – 'to drift', etc. Maybe, as in the case of an extract from *The Crossing* by Kathy Watson, some aspect of nature has been personified to belittle the scale and efforts of human beings: '…a stream powered by the North Sea would sweep him south-west.'

J SYMPATHISE WITH:

A writer can elicit our sympathy by using emotive words – 'poor', for instance – and by repeating these words for emphasis. They can also elicit sympathy by personifying something. For instance, in an extract about a kookaburra, the kookaburra is killed by a boy's slingshot. The kookaburra is personified as being a 'brother', a 'friend', to make the crime seem all the more terrible. The writer also evokes our sympathy by contrasting the death with a preceding paragraph describing how happy and tuneful the bird was before.

3 ANALYSING POETRY

This resource helps pupils to approach an unseen poem methodically, using three logical steps to decipher meaning, tone and the way that stanzas, rhythm, rhyme and language choices contribute to understanding.

If the techniques are learnt and habitually applied to every poem, confidence is developed for approaching poems independently.

Developing the habit of working logically through these steps **before** reading any subsequent questions prepares pupils effectively and builds confidence and independence.

Poems referred to:

Child on Top of a Greenhouse by Theodore Roethke
The Tyger by William Blake
Pigeons by Richard Kell
The Listeners by Walter de la Mare

First, read the poem a couple of times and then work through the checklist 'Idea, structure, language'. Overleaf, I discuss what to consider for each item on the checklist.

IDEA

Does the title give you any preconceptions of what the poem will be about?

Where is the poem set? When is it set? What is the weather like?

Who is speaking?

Mark off each sentence (the end of a sentence is marked by one of three punctuation symbols: a full stop, an exclamation mark or a question mark). Do you understand what each sentence means?

What is the tone/mood of the poem? Is it the same throughout, or does it change? If so, where?

Are there moments of drama? Contrast? Transition? If so, where?

 STRUCTURE

How many stanzas/verses are there? Do they look the same as each other in terms of length and shape? If so, why? If not, why? If only one stanza, how many lines?

Is there a rhyme scheme? If so, what is it in terms of 'abc'?

Count the syllables. Is there a regular rhythm? If so, consider why. If not, consider why.

For instance, in the poem *Child on Top of a Greenhouse*, there is no regular rhyme or rhythm. This is perhaps because the poet wants to convey a feeling of instability and unpredictability.

However, in William Blake's poem *The Tyger*, the rhyme scheme (aabb) and rhythm are regular to evoke, perhaps, the animal's movement and energy.

Note the use of punctuation. In *Child on Top of a Greenhouse*, the final line finishes with an exclamation mark to stress the child's embarrassment, perhaps, at being the focus of attention.

Note also whether sentences are continued across lines or stanzas, which is called **enjambment**. This technique may be used to suggest a lack of control or form.

LANGUAGE/DICTION

This refers to the poet's choice of words and descriptive techniques.

Patterns

Note any patterns of language or diction.
For instance, the **nouns** in *Child on Top of a Greenhouse* include:

> *wind, seat, britches, feet, splinters, glass,*
> *putty, chrysanthemums, accusers, sunlight,*
> *clouds, elms, horses, everyone*

The **verbs** include:

> *to billow, to crackle, to stare, to flash, to*
> *rush, to plunge, to toss, to point, to shout*

Some of those verbs evoke the wind's energy; others evoke the child's sense of persecution, perhaps.

Repetition

Are any words repeated? In *Child on Top of a Greenhouse*, the word 'everyone' is repeated in the line:

> *'And everyone, everyone pointing up*
> *and shouting!'*

This serves to emphasise the child's discomfort, perhaps, at being the main focus of attention.

Imagery/figurative language

Note the use of imagery/figurative language. Are there any similes? In a *Child on Top of the Greenhouse*, the speaker makes a direct comparison:

> *'A line of elms plunging and tossing*
> *like horses'*

This simile is effective because it makes us think of wild, unpredictable and restless horses, and so we envisage the trees billowing and waving in a strong wind.

Also, the speaker describes the 'half-crown chrysanthemums staring up like accusers'. This simile implies the child's unease about being the focus of attention.

Metaphors

Are there any metaphors? For instance, in the poem *Pigeons* by Richard Kell, the pigeons are described as 'fat gentlemen with hands clasped beneath swallowtail coats'.

This is **personification**, a common form of metaphor. By comparing the pigeons to 'fat gentlemen', the poet creates a picture of the pigeons' protruding chests. The 'swallowtail' coats convey a grey and white colour scheme and the bird's folded-back wings are conveyed by reference to the gentlemen's hands being clasped behind their backs.

3

Senses

Has the poet made reference to different senses – hearing, seeing, smelling, tasting and feeling – to bring their writing to life? Sometimes writers will refer directly to what they can see and hear; other times they can be more subtle.

For instance, writers will use various techniques for hearing/feeling, such as **alliteration**, **assonance** and **onomatopoeia**.

In Walter de la Mare's poem *The Listeners*, the phrase 'forest's ferny floor' is an example of alliteration. The repetition of the soft 'f' sounds evokes the soft surface of the forest's floor.

In *Child on Top of a Greenhouse*, the words 'wind', 'billowing', 'britches' and 'splinters' echo the same short internal 'i' sound, an example of assonance. The effect is to create the repetitive airiness of the wind's nagging strength, perhaps.

Also in *Child on Top of a Greenhouse*, onomatopoeia in the form of sibilants ('s' sounds) is used – for example, 'tossing like horses'. The repetition of the 's' sounds echoes the sound of the wind in the trees.

4 PLANNING FOR WRITING

Planning creative writing tasks is something many pupils find difficult, especially in exam conditions. Pupils can feel overwhelmed by thinking that 'planning' should be a synopsis of what they plan to write. Instead, planning can be a process of assembling the vital ingredients required for good writing.

Good writing is controlled. Good writing is expressed through accurate and varied sentence structures organised into a series of paragraphs with different focuses. Good writing uses techniques (set out in these pages) that evoke mood, atmosphere and characterisation. Good writing is well crafted.

The following resource is one we developed in our classroom. It provides a systematic checklist of things to be included in your writing – whatever the genre.

The items on the checklist are organised under the following headings:

IDEA

WHO, WHEN, WHERE, WEATHER

STYLE AND FORM

VOCABULARY

As soon as you've chosen your prompt, organise your thoughts under these headings or headings of your own choice. The important thing is to consider all these different facets as part of your planning. Overleaf, I discuss what to consider for each heading.

A IDEA

The first thing you need to do is decide what you are going to write and the aim behind it. What will be your beginning, middle and end? Will you use a chronological structure or do you want to reorder events into a flashback or use a narrative frame (a story within a story)?

Think about giving your writing texture by including moments of drama, contrast and transition.

Remember that 'drama' can simply refer to moments when your characters move. Writing which is driven by a series of melodramatic events tends to be unrealistic. Writing in which the action is restrained and interspersed with techniques for creating mood, atmosphere and characterisation can be more powerful and engaging.

'Contrast' may refer to moments when characters react differently to one another or to when characters or settings look different at different times.

'Transition' may refer to interesting moments of growth or deterioration in a character or situation.

When planning your ideas, imagine yourself as a film director organising a string of scenes in the best order for telling the story clearly. Allow your camera to hover on different areas or on characters' faces. Let your camera explore its surroundings – the distant views and the detailed close-ups.

B WHO, WHERE, WHEN, WEATHER

Whether you are writing about a place, a person, an exciting event or a personal experience, consider the following first:

- Who? (Who are the people present or involved?)
- Where? (Urban or rural?)
- When? (Season/morning/noon/night?) Keep the time frame simple and short.
- Weather? (Wind, rain, snow, sunshine, mist or just a flat, grey, nondescript sort of day?)

C STYLE AND FORM

You need to demonstrate your ability to:

- Vary sentence types (simple, compound and complex) according to mood and atmosphere. Remember that short sentences create tension and longer sentences create a more flowing rhythm (see page 80).

- Maintain a consistent verb tense (past or present) and consistent narrative voice (first person or third person).

- Have different focuses for different paragraphs (weather, senses, shift in time, shift in perspective, dialogue and characterisation, for instance).

- Punctuate dialogue correctly (see page 92).

- Use dialogue as a tool for developing character and mood.

If you vary the way you **start** your sentences, you will prompt yourself to use different types of sentences and phrases:

Adverb starter

Gingerly, she eased the letter from its envelope.
Suddenly, a pheasant exploded from the undergrowth.
Furtively, he peered into the cupboard and slipped a Haribo into his pocket.

Prepositional phrase

At the end of the lane, ...
Beyond the swaying poplars, ...
Beneath the window, ...
Under my fingertips, ...

Present participle

Entering the yard, ...
Stumbling through the doorway, ...
Pausing to catch her breath, ...

Lists

Lists are an excellent way to create a stronger sense of setting or atmosphere:

I could hear nothing but the persistent tick of the grandfather clock, a log hissing and shifting in the grate and the wind whining at the kitchen door.

She packed her bags hastily, stuffing in an old green jersey of her father's, two pairs of jeans, assorted socks and her favourite yellow pyjamas. She forgot her toothbrush, toothpaste, soap and a towel, as was her habit.

D VOCABULARY

All good writing contains descriptive techniques which enrich the language and enable readers to see and feel the scenes the writer is trying to convey. In your planning time, consider the following:

PRECISE DICTION (NOUNS, VERBS, ADJECTIVES, ADVERBS, ETC)

Once you have chosen your setting, write down as many **nouns** as you can think of to do with that setting. If it's a seascape, for instance: yachts, ferries, dinghies, port, harbour, quay, cottages, lighthouse, sea, sand, shingle, cliffs, seagulls. Try to use them all to bring your setting into sharper focus.

If you can see or hear 'birds', be specific. If you are setting your writing in England, for instance, choose birds which are indigenous to the English countryside – robins, blackbirds, buzzards, crows, sparrows. Think of their behaviour and their tunes.

- **Robins** hop; they sing.
- **Blackbirds** sing, usually on their own, from the tops of trees – especially in the evening.
- **Buzzards** float and wheel high up in the sky; they mew.
- **Crows** caw and cackle raucously.
- **Sparrows** chatter.
- **Larks** flutter high above the ground.

Also choose specific trees/hedgerows which are indigenous to the countryside:

- Oaks
- Sycamores
- Poplars
- Holly
- Brambles
- Nettles
- Elderflower blossom

This creates atmospheric detail and allows you to explore and develop your surroundings.

Once you have chosen your weather type – rain, sun, cloud, wind, fog, frost, snow – choose the **verbs** associated with that weather type. For example, if you have chosen rain, jot down verbs such as: drizzle, patter, drip or cascade, bombard, gush or hammer.

Think about giving the weather type a personality. Heavy rain could be a destructive bully, while a gentle, maternal breeze could soothe, whisper, stroke, ruffle or gently rock.

Remember to avoid the bland 'big', 'little' adjectives and don't use adjectives for the sake of them. Most of the time, the precise use of nouns and verbs creates a strong picture. However, used imaginatively, adjectives are an excellent tool for creating extra detail. The same applies to adverbs. You can see this in the following extract from *Walking Home* by Simon Armitage:

> *'There's also a **village** hall – a **tidy**, **black-and-white-painted**, **stone-built**, **slate-roofed** construction – at the heart of the settlement'*

SENSES

What, in my location, can I see, feel, hear, smell, taste?

SOUND

A useful technique for incorporating sound is 'the list of three':

> I could hear nothing but the steady drum of rain on the glass roof, the sound of my own breathing and, distantly, a car changing gear on the lane.

Another useful technique for conveying sound is onomatopoeia. Notice the onomatopoeic quality of the 's's to evoke the rustling sound in this sentence:

> The evening breeze sighed through the leaves and rustled the long grasses.

Another way to evoke and emphasise sound is alliteration:

> **P**inpricks of **p**ale light **p**enetrated the gloom. **R**oads and **r**ailway tracks **r**an in all directions.

SIMILES AND METAPHORS

Worse than not including any similes and metaphors is to overuse them, but similes used sparingly create clear images.

> 'His eyes rolled like marbles at the bottom of a pail'
> (simile from *Thursday's Child* by Sonya Hartnett)

> 'Needles of daylight stabbed the gloom of the basement through holes in a wooden trap door'
> (metaphor from *Once* by Morris Gleitzman)

Personification is a form of metaphor that brings writing to life. Personify the weather you have chosen:

> The November wind howled through the treetops and moaned around the yard.

> Warm fingers of sunshine caressed the back of her neck and played with her hair.

> The cold pinched his fingertips and wouldn't let go.

ARCHIE'S PLANNING FOR WRITING

In exam conditions, Archie independently applied the checklist from the Planning for Writing resource to produce an effective piece of timed writing entitled 'The Picnic'.

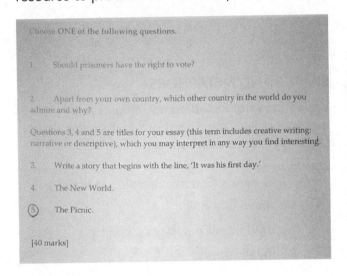

'THE PICNIC', BY ARCHIE

I could feel the rays of June sunshine on my back. I darted about the park moving under the oak trees, with their crisp green leaves, and brushing past hedges and gleaming grass. The sky was a bubbly blue and not a cloud was above to spoil it. The trees swayed to the wind's melody and a pleasant breeze washed over me. It felt like a dream.

Stopping, I smelt an indescribable scent. I zoomed towards it, hovering beneath the engulfing trees. I perched on a bench and peered about the park to find the source of the delicious smells. Dogs travelled past, kids chased and played and the flowers made a paint palette before my eyes. Suddenly, I saw it. A large family with children eating fruit and the now recognisable smell of... jam. I couldn't resist going closer.

I ducked below the bench and dived towards them, landing on a sandwich.

Suddenly, the alarm was raised. Large palms came flying towards me. The children dropped their food and fled in terror. I evaded the wrinkled hands of grandparents but books and flasks of coffee were swung at me. I flew past faces and hid under the folds of their blankets. I could tell I was creating a buzz.

From my position, I could sense the parents hunting for me. It was time to get out with what little loot I had gained. I zipped away only to be stopped by a hedge of needle-like branches and razor-sharp leaves. My black and yellow jumpsuit shook as I dodged another attempt on my life from the father. I needed to escape. The children's voices were shrill sirens, getting louder as I buzzed towards them. Once again, they fled in terror. This was my chance.

I squeezed through a gap in the needle-like branches just as I could feel another hand swing down. I was out. I panted heavily, sucking in gulps of air. I could still smell the jam, so I buzzed off, not to be tempted again. My wings gesticulated frantically and crumbs flew everywhere. I knew never again to pillage or even visit the stronghold they call 'The Picnic'.

SONGS AS A STIMULUS

With an essay title like 'Flight', for example, the temptation is for pupils to write accounts of being at the airport about to jet off on a family holiday. This isn't wrong but it can be difficult to avoid writing a tedious 'And then… And then…' account of events. Try to encourage pupils to think laterally and metaphorically about a title.

We approached the essay stimulus 'Flight' by thinking first of the language associated with bird flight. This gave rise to words and phrases such as 'spreading the wings', 'leaving the nest', 'soaring', 'freedom', etc., which we gathered on the board.

Then we listened to the Beatles' song *She's Leaving Home* (you can find the lyrics online). We absorbed the lyrics, which are very clearly defined to provide a strong narrative framework.

The pupils enjoyed listening to the music and discussing relationships, misunderstandings, rhyme schemes and rhythms, and the parents' transition from indignation to soul-searching. This, combined with the language already gathered for flight, gave them the framework for writing a metaphorical piece about a girl leaving home. The pupils rose to the challenge well.

Here is Archie's piece:

'FLIGHT', BY ARCHIE

4.00am. A peaceful breeze drifts down the lane. Floating, it circles around dustbins, rustling the black plastic. At the end of the road, the wind flies – soaring through trees and bushes until playing a sudden tune on wind chimes outside a small suburban house.

A light flicks on, illuminating the street, highlighting early December's sugary frost. Through the window is a teenage girl, pulling on a grey woollen sweater and shoving various items into her backpack: crisps, iPhone, a hoodie, a hat, a scarf and much more. On her bed is a black coat with a fur-lined hood. She lifts the hood and brushes strands of black hair out of her face.

With an unexpected click of the lock, the girl opens her door and the hallway embraces the light. Her boots creak on the floor as she scribbles down a note and sticks it on the bannister. Pulling her rucksack onto her back, she drifts, gingerly, down the stairs. She can feel herself leaving her nest, the nest that had confined her to solitude for years. As she unlocks the front door, she spreads her wings. Once through the door, she feels her spirit soaring into the night.

The door slams and her parents awake.

Tying the knot on her dressing gown, sliding on her slippers, Mother opens the door and sees the note. A few seconds pass, as she processes the words. At once, she breaks down in tears, slumped at the top of the stairs. Her husband leaps up and runs to his wife to comfort her. They sit, grounded, as she soars into the outside world, leaving her captors behind.

Another song with a strong narrative structure and which gives rise to interesting discussions about homelessness and philanthropy is Phil Collins' *Another Day in Paradise*. It can also provide a confidence-inspiring template for creative writing.

Here is Dora's piece:

'ANOTHER DAY IN PARADISE', BY DORA

The rain drummed on the rooftops and crept down windows, angry car-horns beeped and disgruntled pedestrians took cover. Umbrellas rose and so did tempers. The bustling city was a blizzard of colour and sound. And as she stood all alone, sodden and shivering, her bare arms stinging and her fearful heart beating, she searched the crowd for a friendly face and found none. Her eyes filled with tears, but no one so much as glanced at her; her frail body was insignificant in the mass of movement and noise.

Bodies and voices rushed past her, towering above her fragile head. Feet pounced into puddles and filthy water splashed into her tear-stained face. Defeated, she sat down against a wall daubed with graffiti and closed her eyes. No one noticed her, and no one came for her as she sat, shivering, fighting off the dread.

But when the streets had cleared and the crowds had gone, she remained, her clothes sodden through and her blue lips frozen. Not a flicker of life was left in her. Her frail body, still and cold, stayed there and nobody noticed.

6 POETRY AS A STIMULUS

PORPHYRIA'S LOVER BY ROBERT BROWNING

The rain set early in to-night,
    The sullen wind was soon awake,
It tore the elm-tops down for spite,
    And did its worst to vex the lake:
    I listened with heart fit to break.
When glided in Porphyria; straight
    She shut the cold out and the storm,
And kneeled and made the cheerless grate
    Blaze up, and all the cottage warm;
    Which done, she rose, and from her form
Withdrew the dripping cloak and shawl,
    And laid her soiled gloves by, untied
Her hat and let the damp hair fall,
    And, last, she sat down by my side
    And called me. When no voice replied,
She put my arm about her waist,
    And made her smooth white shoulder bare,
And all her yellow hair displaced,
    And, stooping, made my cheek lie there,
    And spread, o'er all, her yellow hair,
Murmuring how she loved me — she
    Too weak, for all her heart's endeavour,
To set its struggling passion free
    From pride, and vainer ties dissever,
    And give herself to me for ever.
But passion sometimes would prevail,
    Nor could to-night's gay feast restrain
A sudden thought of one so pale
    For love of her, and all in vain:
    So, she was come through wind and rain.

Be sure I looked up at her eyes
    Happy and proud; at last I knew
Porphyria worshipped me; surprise
    Made my heart swell, and still it grew
    While I debated what to do.
That moment she was mine, mine, fair,
    Perfectly pure and good: I found
A thing to do, and all her hair
    In one long yellow string I wound
    Three times her little throat around,
And strangled her. No pain felt she;
    I am quite sure she felt no pain.
As a shut bud that holds a bee,
    I warily oped her lids: again
    Laughed the blue eyes without a stain.
And I untightened next the tress
    About her neck; her cheek once more
Blushed bright beneath my burning kiss:
    I propped her head up as before,
    Only, this time my shoulder bore
Her head, which droops upon it still:
    The smiling rosy little head,
So glad it has its utmost will,
    That all it scorned at once is fled,
    And I, its love, am gained instead!
Porphyria's love: she guessed not how
    Her darling one wish would be heard.
And thus we sit together now,
    And all night long we have not stirred,
    And yet God has not said a word!

A group of pupils studying *Porphyria's Lover* researched some facts about Browning first and interesting discussions ensued about the difference between the monologues (for which Browning was famous) and the soliloquys.

We read the poem, applying the systematic checklist provided in the Analysing Poetry resource. The pupils enjoyed the 'dark humour'.

We divided the poem up into sections, which became separate paragraph focuses for a piece of creative writing in which pupils applied contemporary issues while emulating the narrative structure of Browning's poem. Being given permission to be violent was popular(!) and the exercise helped to develop pupils' craftsmanship.

We wrote our pieces in class together, allowing ourselves 5-6 minutes for each paragraph, and then compared the results. Not only did pupils enjoy the exercise and the peer evaluation which followed, but they also learnt to have an open mind about poetry from the past in which archaic language and syntax is used.

Here is Seb's piece of writing:

Robert's friend

The early morning lemon sun stained the pale blue sky, its golden fountains trickling down onto St Hugh's school. A peaceful veil was draped around the countryside and they was not a fluffy cloud in sight. A warm breeze gushed in and out of the window, like the breath of an animal. Wonderful...

I listened to the soft sweet chirps of a song thrush outside, with joy in my heart.

Suddenly the door swung open and Robert stormed into the room, threw his already battered schoolbag against the wall and slumped sheepishly into the chair next to mine... Tension seized the lonely classroom.

He told me he was going to leave school because of his father's new job, he was too weak against the words of his parents and was helpless to fight his case. I told him how I would never forget him and how he would always be my friend, but envy of his new friends swirled inside me like a swamp.

A sudden thought pulled at me like a huge tentacle, I saw him with a gang of new people, his character was different from the boy I knew. My thoughts swirled back and tears blurred my vision, I wiped them away and caught one in my hand. It looked like some mythical birds egg and I watched as it slid around my palm. Robert then ran and hugged me and at last I knew he needed me. A strange feeling swelled inside my chest as I debated what to do, in that moment he was my friend. I found a thing to do

I picked up his A4 sheet and scrumpled it up, then I stuffed it down his throat, he did not say anything long, he choked on his words.

His face stared back at mine, his glassy eyes glazed over, he watched me as I sat back down and carried on writing in the empty classroom, he was preserved in the moment. An eerie silence swallowed the school.

7 A POETRY/PROSE TEMPLATE FOR EXPLORING EMOTIONS

To encourage pupils to 'hover the camera' on a particular idea and develop it, rather than feel they must keep everything moving forward, we created this resource.

CHOOSE AN EMOTION:

- Anger
- Happiness/joy
- Fear
- Jealousy
- Revulsion
- Sadness
- Disgust
- Embarrassment
- Loneliness
- Conceit
- Pride
- Arrogance
- Nervousness
- Disgrace
- Disappointment
- Anxiety

TASK FOR PUPILS:

Work through the questions below using the emotion of your choice (I will provide examples for anger):

What colour is your emotion?

> *(Anger is purple and red. Like a flash of flame or an open wound)*

What time of day is it?

> *(Anger is the creeping transition from day to night – dusk)*

What season is anger?

> *(Anger is winter – February. It is a long, dark night)*

What type of weather is it?

> *(Anger is a howling wind that rattles windows and destroys buildings and rips the branches off trees)*

If it were a musical instrument, what would it be?

> *(Anger is a crashing cymbal that rings in my ears and reverberates around the room/my head)*

If it were a piece of furniture, what would it be?

> *(Anger is the door of the furnace – burning and blistering)*

CREATE A POEM OR A PIECE OF PROSE USING YOUR IDEAS

Poem

Anger.

Purple and red.

Like a flash of flame; an opening wound.

The creeping transition from day to night – dusk.

Anger is a howling wind that rattles windows
and destroys buildings;
it rips the branches off trees.
It is a crashing cymbal that rings in my ears
and reverberates around my head.

Anger is the top of the hob,
burning and blistering.

Prose

Cynthia felt angry. It erupted inside her, purple and red, like an open wound. She had tried so hard to contain it, to feel calm and level-headed, but the provocation overwhelmed her and she felt the creeping transition from day to night, the dusk before the dark howling wind of emotion that rattled her nerves and nagged and niggled her inner voice of reason.

She was suddenly a seething mass of vengeance and spite. She shouted and her voice rang and reverberated in the kitchen as though a cymbal had been crashed. The effect on Tom was instant. He flinched as though he'd placed his bare hand on the electric hob.

Here is Darcy's poem:

> **'JEALOUSY', BY DARCY**
>
> It's a sickly green
> Like 6am on a Monday morning.
> Exhausting.
> It crawls under your skin like a bug and, like a tumour, it grows and grows until you either treat it or fulfil its malicious desire.
> It's an out of tune violin playing half-hearted Mozart.
> The feeling of spite is like the short days and icy cold rain in early February.
> Jealousy blurs your vision.
> Making you unable to see right from wrong.
> Like a boy adrift at sea without a map or compass.
> It's an old forgotten porcelain vase that was once admired but now stands in the corner Ignored. Begging for attention.
> It's controlling, manipulative and ruthless.
> Jealousy is a mosquito
> Sly and biting, leaving a mark even when it's long gone.

8 SHAKESPEARE AS A STIMULUS

A group of pupils studied *A Midsummer Night's Dream* in the summer term. We looked at Oberon's monologue (Act 2, Scene 1):

I know a bank where the wild thyme blows,
Where oxlips and the nodding violet grows,
Quite over-canopied with luscious woodbine,
With sweet musk-roses and with eglantine:
There sleeps Titania sometime of the night,
Lull'd in these flowers with dances and delight;
And there the snake throws her enamell'd skin,
Weed wide enough to wrap a fairy in: …

We used this as a structure or framework for writing about pupils' own favourite places. Here are Theo and Ben's interpretations:

'I KNOW A PLACE…', BY THEO

I know a dune where sand flows freely,
Where empty miles stretch and where the
sand is smooth like velvet and
forms mounds.
I know a place where a single tree stands
strong in a sea of sand.
There will you find camels cowering from the
unforgiving wind and scalding heat.
I know a room where the dirt thrives.
Where books colonise the corners like settlers.
Quite over-canopied with open drawers
and bulging cupboards.
Here dust settles in every crevice and
There I sleep in a kingdom over-run with lost
toys and debris.

'I KNOW A PLACE…', BY BEN

I know a place where the mayfly drifts
Where streaming water weeds float and
vicious nettles' spears sting
Where, beneath the rippling surface,
fat trout tremor.
Quite over-arched with wandering willows'
arms,
Here, underfoot, boggy mud squelches
And there glides the mallard with orange
flappers and shiny green neck
And, hidden in the bank, the fisherman's lair

9 CREATING ORIGINAL MATERIAL COLLABORATIVELY

Sometimes, it's difficult for a teacher to find a piece of writing which demonstrates the learning objectives.

Writing something in collaboration with pupils to highlight techniques is a potent way to show the creative process. Pupils benefit greatly from seeing that writing evolves, paragraph by paragraph, and that, just like them, you cannot always find the right phrase immediately. They learn that by re-reading and experimenting with the rhythms of sentences, ideas unfold.

In the autumn term, a group of pupils studied *A Christmas Carol* by Charles Dickens, culminating in an opportunity to write their own ghost stories.

Overleaf is a ghost story worksheet written for the pupils. Included afterwards is a chilling ghost story written by Alfred; it arose from the worksheet and the ideas we discussed.

The Ghost Story worksheet

Other words for ghosts include:

spirits, spectres, apparitions

phantoms, shadows, souls

Traditionally, ghosts are people who have died but whose spirits/souls live on to haunt those living.

Ghosts make people feel afraid because they have supernatural powers: they can glide through locked doors, disappear and make noises or alter things without our permission.

Ghosts are unwelcome presences in houses because they are unpredictable and because we feel powerless in their presence.

The sudden appearance/presence of a ghost can create a great deal of tension.

Tension can be created in various ways:

- **Short sentences** = a staccato rhythm.
- **Dim lighting** = creates shadows.
- **Adverbs at the beginning of sentences** = inject a sudden change of pace.
- **Dismemberment** = withholding someone's identity or reducing them to a series of body parts/features (voices, hands, footsteps) creates a sense of mystery.
- **Holding up the action** = create tension with ellipses (…), a focus on sensory information, a countdown.
- **Referring to a typical human response to fear** = clammy hands, dry mouth, beating heart.
- **Verbs which suggest stealthiness** = tiptoe, whisper, creep.

Characterisation

Ghosts, like other characters in stories, need the same elements to bring them to 'life': a physical description, objects associated with them, behaviour, what they say or don't say, how others react to them, clothing and, to emulate the ghosts in Dickens' *A Christmas Carol*, you can include 'the strangest thing' about them.

Our ghost story

Paragraph 1: as with any piece of descriptive writing, it is important to choose a weather type as this can be the way into a story.

It was December. Only one week left of the autumn term. Everyone was exhausted, staff and pupils alike. Jane Seymour was on late-night duty, which she dreaded as it meant locking the school up at 8.30 before going home. That night, the school was sprinkled with a covering of sparkling salt. Frost had descended and held St Hugh's and its environment in its steel-like grip. Up on the playing fields, the grass was blades of silver daggers and icicles hung from the Pavilion. Around the Tom Young Building, everything was lit by a bright moon in a dark sky studded with stars. Jane set out, the bunch of heavy school keys jangling in her hand, to lock up. She felt at her most apprehensive around the Barn. There the shadows were particularly sinister, and Jane had to stifle thoughts of leather-gloved hands grabbing her from behind.

Paragraph 2: using the senses.

Distantly, Jane could hear an owl screeching in the woods and from the boarding house windows she could hear muffled laughter. The children were going to their dormitories and so Jane was alone outside. She crouched over the band of keys struggling to find the one labelled 'Barn'. Her hands were stiff with cold and her nose felt numb, but soon the dreaded task would be over and she could drive back to the warmth of her own home. Despite an inner voice which urged Jane to be calm, she felt frightened. She had a distinct sense that something was nearby and that something or somebody was watching her silently from the freezing shadows.

Paragraph 3: shifting the focus; exploring the surroundings.

Very slowly, she willed herself to turn around and flash her torch into the darkness. The yellow triangle of light played across the entrance to the new Cannon building, over the arch into the swimming pool, up into the skeletal branches of the pear tree and down across the silvery path that led to the sports hall. Nothing unusual was there but still Jane felt anxious. Her mouth was dry and her heart was beating in her chest. She had heard something, something akin to breathing nearby.

Paragraph 4: the ghost.

When Jane whipped around, she did not really expect to see anything, but there, in front of her very eyes, was a figure. No taller than a child but wizened, like an old man, its eyes were dark pools in a face of white marble. It wore the clothes of a child from Dickensian times – a cap, britches, braces and stockings – but the strangest thing about it was that it was smiling, and the smile was not sinister but gentle and kind. Jane's fear evaporated. The apparition appeared to want her to follow it as it held its white hand out to her and nodded its ghostly head. Jane felt drawn to it, as if being asked to follow her own mother. It was an extraordinarily compelling feeling. No longer did she feel cold, but a warmth spread through her as though she had just drunk a sip of mulled wine. Glancing back at the unlocked door of the Barn, Jane wavered. She hesitated and in that instant of indecision, something very strange happened. The spirit disappeared into the thin frosty air.

Paragraph 5: the evidence.

Had she been dreaming? Why was she not scared? Jane shook her head in disbelief. Something was glinting in the moonlight. She stooped to pick it up and looked at the palm of her hand.

Within her hand was an ancient badge – the motto on it clearly visible still. It was the motto of St Hugh's and the date on the badge was 1800.

A GHOST STORY, BY ALFRED

The children had finished their activity for the evening and were going up to bed. I was not allowed to leave for home because I was on boarding duty and had to lock up. I put my wool hat and gloves on and left the sports hall. Frost was sprinkled all around school like sugar and clung to the ground firmly. Icicles hung from the gutters. The leaves looked as if they had been heaped with sea salt and when you kicked them, droplets of magic dispersed into the air. The naked trees reached out proudly towards the dark sky.

A satisfying wave went through my body when I knew that I had finished locking up all the buildings and I knew I could go home. I went up the frosted steps towards matron and entered into the warm Manor House. Underneath me I heard what I thought was a piano playing. I rubbed my ear but I still heard it. It was coming from the cold, dark music rooms. All the children had gone up and the music teachers had gone home. I saw my shadow against the wall in the corridor; it looked as if somebody else was walking up the stairs towards me.

Distantly the music repeated again and again. As I walked closer, the music became louder and my heart thumped in my chest. I never believed in supernatural beings or ghosts and I never will. So why was I scared? Who was playing the tune? I tried to calm myself by saying to myself – it is just someone messing around, it is just someone messing around. There was one room left in the corridor that was Mrs Havelock's room, on the left. I always thought of it as being the coldest and darkest room. I approached it but as I started to turn the handle I saw some hair and I stumbled backwards toward the wall and regathered myself. It is just someone messing around, I repeated under my breath. This time it did not reassure me.

I took a deep breath and walked in. I opened my mouth to shout but nothing came. A young girl of about nine or ten sat at the piano. She had long grey hair as if with age but a smooth white face. She was barefoot. Although the strangest thing about her was she had no eyes, just darkness where they would be, she carried on playing. I opened the door again and was about to run when she twisted her head, without moving her body, like an owl. She simply stared at me. Well she would have done if she had eyes. All she did was raise her finger to her lips and gently said, 'Shhhhhh.'

10 MOOD, ATMOSPHERE AND CHARACTERISATION

As an example of a piece of writing that 'pays particular attention to mood, atmosphere and characterisation', I wrote the Harry Pendelbury piece. It was a great favourite with pupils, who still want to know what happens next.

'HARRY PENDELBURY', BY SARAH NORTH

Paragraph 1: set the scene and tone using weather to explore your surroundings.

It was raining and not just spitting rain but a torrential, almost tropical downpour. Harry Pendelbury sheltered in the doorway of the Plaza hotel and watched the New York traffic splash past him on Fifth Avenue. He glanced at his watch. It was only 4 o'clock but already it was nearly dark even for the time of year. Three weeks to Christmas. The vista before him was a blur of bright festive lights. Harry thrust his hands deep into his coat pockets and shivered. He was dreading going home.

Paragraph 2: alter the focus. What is going on inside the character's head?

The interview had not gone well. In front of a panel of four judges in a mahogany panelled board room, Harry had felt intimidated. The questions about his home life had made him squirm and translating that document into Russian had flummoxed him. Harry had been well out of his comfort zone. Now he would have to face the music and confess his shortcomings to his wife.

Paragraph 3: introduce the senses.

Rainwater seeped into the soles of his shoes and the winter wind snaked around his ankles and tugged at his coat. People were bustling past, heads down, their shoulders dragged downwards by the weight of bags of Christmas shopping. Tinny Christmas music drifted out of shop doors and a figure in a reindeer costume, its antlers soaked by the downpour, shook his charity can half-heartedly at the flow of pedestrians but they didn't take any notice of him.

Paragraph 4: introduce characterisation with a physical description, objects associated with the character, their behaviour, others' behaviour towards them, what they say and think.

At 35, Harry Pendelbury still had the look of a shy boy. He was tall with a small head and neat fair hair. His features were delicate although his mouth was full. He glanced again at his watch. It had been a present from his father and Harry felt a stab of loss when he looked at its classic square face and neat Roman numbers. His briefcase had been passed down to him by his grandfather. It was old but the leather was still good, and he had maintained it with regular daubs of saddle soap. 'I wish they were both still alive. They believed in me,' he thought despondently, shrugging his neck deep into his collar. Despite himself, tears of self-pity pricked his eyes, but no one would have noticed. They were all too preoccupied.

Paragraph 5: introduce some action and finish. An ending does not necessarily require resolution. It can, as here, leave a sense of mystery…

His hands closed around his mobile phone. Should he ring again? She said she'd come to collect him, but she was twenty minutes late. How would he break the news? How would he be able to say that, again, he'd failed and see the look of scorn and disappointment in her face. He glanced up and down the road and on the instant, made a decision. He turned out of the hotel and slipped unnoticed into the stream of passers-by. He walked briskly and purposefully into the fast-moving current of Christmas shoppers without a backward glance.

FINAL TASK

Continue the piece of writing. What happens to Harry Pendelbury?

Good luck!

APPENDIX: ANSWERS AND SUGGESTED RESPONSES

ANSWERS AND SUGGESTED RESPONSES

1. NOUNS

Word	Word class	Meaning
crickets	noun	jumping insects that make loud noises by rubbing their wings
demented	adjective	behaving irrationally through distress
to attain	verb	to achieve/to accomplish
to stomp	verb	to tread heavily (or angrily)
an array	noun	an impressive display or range of things
statistician	noun	an expert who analyses statistics
busker	noun	a street performer
Camembert	noun	a creamy French cheese with a strong, pungent smell

NOUNS: TASK 1

The midday *sun* [common] burnt the back of her *legs* [common] and the *crickets* [common] in the French

countryside [common] sounded like a demented *gaggle of geese* [collective]. She wanted to swim

in the *pool* [common] but her English *homework* [common] beckoned and, as her *mum* [common] kept telling

her, *knowledge* [abstract] was not inherited but attained through hard *work* [common]. She had

been threatened with poor *reports* [common] from the *Headmaster* [proper] but even this couldn't

persuade her that *swimming* [common] was not a preferable *option* [abstract] to studying *nouns* [common].

Caroline [proper] sighed. Her *brother* [common] stomped past carrying an *array of swimming pool* [collective]

gear [common]. From behind his *mask* [common], he smirked at her and, though he was already

wearing his *snorkel* [common], she made out his *words* [common]: 'You're being watched. *A crowd of* [collective]

headmasters is coming for you.' *World War III* [proper] was about to erupt.

NOUNS: TASK 2

For this task you could write something like:

The setting of this passage is a school. This is conveyed by the noun choices, which include 'term', 'sports hall', 'wall bars', 'a vault', 'a climbing frame', 'ropes' and 'pupil'.

NOUNS: TASK 3

For this task you could write something like:

The setting of this passage is a ski resort. This is conveyed by the noun choices, which include 'skiing holiday', 'chalet', 'ski clothes', 'helmet', 'ski suit', 'moon boots' and 'ski scarf'.

NOUNS: TASK 4

Your list of nouns associated with 'The Harbour' might include:

Sea, tide, beach, children, buckets and spades, dogs, ferry, fishing boats, balls, sailing boats, lighthouse, hotels, pubs, restaurants, cottages, passengers, headland, seagulls, buoys, quay, harbour wall, bay.

I used my list of nouns to write the following piece:

The Easter sun shimmered on the Cornish sea. The tide was up, hiding the yellow strip of beach beneath the harbour wall where, when the tide was out, small children played with their buckets and spades and dogs fetched balls. Sailing boats bobbed on their buoys and, beside the quay, the ferry, alongside a fleet of fishing boats, was taking passengers. The seaside buildings – hotels, pubs, restaurants and white-washed cottages – looked seawards across the bay to the lighthouse on the distant headland. Overhead, seagulls circled and squawked.

2. ADJECTIVES

Word	Word class	Meaning
poplars	noun	tall, deciduous trees
doddery	adjective	slow and unsteady (with age)
bespectacled	adjective	wearing glasses
cobbled	adjective	paved with cobbles (stones)
explicit	adjective	clear/specific
vague	adjective	uncertain/indefinite/indistinct
writhing	adjective	twisting/squirming movements suggesting discomfort
mogul field	noun	a series of bumps on a ski piste
hysterical	adjective	behaviour that is uncontrolled and emotional

landmark	noun	a feature of the landscape that stands out
frenzy	noun	a state of wild behaviour
competent	adjective	efficient and capable
composed	adjective	under control/calm
irascible	adjective	quick-tempered
timid	adjective	lacking courage/fearful
indignant	adjective	put out/annoyed
effusive	adjective	gushing with praise
hyperbolic	adjective	inclined to exaggeration
obsequious	adjective	overly eager to please

ADJECTIVES: TASK 1A

Mrs Tabitha dressed Moppet and Mittens in clean pinafores and tuckers and then she took out all sorts of elegant, uncomfortable clothes.

ADJECTIVES: TASK 1B

Mrs Tabitha dressed Moppet and Mittens in clean pinafores and tuckers and then she took out all sorts of elegant, uncomfortable clothes.

ADJECTIVES: TASK 1C

The adjectives used in this passage are examples of descriptive adjectives.

The precise use of nouns and adjectives creates a vivid/clear/lively picture.

ADJECTIVES: TASK 2A

First, Mrs Meldrew gathered some shells into her hand. 'These shells came from a beach on an uninhabited island in Italy. Help yourself to these shells, those pencils by the window and that coloured paper on my desk. With this picture as our inspiration, we are going to create a collage using the white glue in that cupboard under the sink.'

ADJECTIVES: TASK 2B

'some', 'these', 'those', 'that' and 'this'

ADJECTIVES: TASK 3A

'I can't hold it,' shrieked Mandy as she wrestled with the boat's helm.

The sails were writhing in the Force 8 gale and the sailing boat was pitching and tossing in the watery mogul field of waves. Mandy was hysterical. Questions flew from her as she struggled to retain her balance. 'Which rope should I pull? What landmark should I follow? Whose charts must I use?'

But it was no use. Her voice was lost in the frenzy of noise.

ADJECTIVES: TASK 3B

Mandy seems to be an inexperienced and panic-stricken sailor. This is apparent from the number of times Mandy uses interrogative adjectives such as 'which', 'what' and 'whose'.

ADJECTIVES: TASK 4

*'Its/It's unfair. **It's/Its** my kitchen, not **hi's/his** and these are **m'y/my** things, not **your/ you're** things. I want my house back!'*

She flung the door back and stomped along the corridor. He could hear her muttering,

*'These people are invading my space with **they're/their** clutter and mess.'*

☑ Irascible   ☐ Frightened   ☑ Possessive   ☐ Timid

The writer has used the possessive adjective 'my' **four times**.

The writer has achieved this effect by

the number of times the possessive adjective 'my' is used: 'my kitchen', 'my things', 'my house' and 'my space'. This has the effect of making the character sound possessive and irascible.

ADJECTIVES: TASK 5

☐ Critical   ☐ Indignant   ☐ Hesitant   ☑ Effusive   ☑ Hyperbolic

The extensive use of superlative adjectives such as 'most delicious', 'spiciest', 'coldest', 'most spectacular' and the use of comparative adjectives such as 'more competent' and 'better time' convey an impression of Christine's appreciation for the lunch she had at Mrs Brown's house. However, the tone of the letter is so effusive that it is in danger of sounding exaggerated and obsequious.

3. VERBS

Word	Word class	Meaning
vigorous	adjective	full of energy
toddler	noun	a child of 1–3 years (still unsteady walking)
carrier	noun	a person who transports people/things
seldom	adjective	rare/not often
rockery	noun	a rock garden
pinafore	noun	an old-fashioned over-garment for protecting clothes
deferential	adjective	showing respect for someone else's views/actions
diplomatic	adjective	sensitive in one's interaction with others
intimidated	adjective	fearful or frightened of something
enthralled	adjective	enchanted or captivated by something
invigorated	adjective	energised
staccato	adjective	jerky rhythm or movement
elusive	adjective	difficult to catch
britches	noun	short trousers fastened below the knee
putty	noun	paste used for sealing glass in a window
chrysanthemums	noun	daisy-like flowers
elms	noun	a type of tree
sobriety	noun	the state of being staid/solemn/serious/measured
to hoard	verb	to gather supplies and secretly guard them
conformist	adjective	sticking to accepted rules and guidelines
defiant	adjective	showing challenging behaviour
eccentric	adjective	slightly strange
conventional	adjective	conforming to usual standards

VERBS: TASK 1

'I was (**to be**) set down from the carrier's cart at the age of three; and there with a sense of bewilderment and terror my life in the village began (**to begin**).

VERBS: TASK 2

1. *I can see the Eiffel Tower from the upstairs window of the apartment.*
2. *Three unemployed youths robbed an elderly lady last Friday.*
3. *Someone has broken the classroom door.*

VERBS: TASK 3

Moppet and Mittens <u>walked</u> down the garden path unsteadily. Presently, they <u>trod</u> upon their pinafores and <u>fell</u> on their noses. When they <u>stood up</u>, there <u>were</u> several green smears.

The extract is written in the <u>past</u> tense.

VERBS: TASK 4

Verb	Infinitive	Present tense	Future tense
walked	to walk	they walk	they will walk
trod	to tread	they tread	they will tread
fell	to fall	they fall	they will fall
stood up	to stand up	they stand up	they will stand up
were	to be	they are	they will be

VERBS: TASK 5

☐ Deferential   ☐ Diplomatic   ☑ Authoritative   ☐ Insecure

☐ Fascinated   ☑ Intimidated   ☐ Enthralled   ☐ Invigorated

VERBS: TASK 6A

For this task you might write something like:

The poem focuses on the appearance and behaviour of pigeons as they move around in large groups in the summer.

VERBS: TASK 6B

For this task you might write something like:

The first stanza focuses very specifically on how the pigeons look and on their movements. The second stanza focuses on the effects of sun on their plumage. The third stanza explores the contented sounds that come from pigeons in the heat of a hot, still summer's day. The atmosphere is slow and heavy until someone makes a sudden movement, like raising their hand, causing the pigeons to take off, as one, into the air.

VERBS: TASK 6C

They <u>paddle</u> with staccato feet
In powder-pools of sunlight,
Small blue busybodies
<u>Strutting</u> like fat gentlemen
With hands <u>clasped</u>
Under their swallowtail coats;
And, as they <u>stump</u> about,
Their heads like tiny hammers
<u>Tap</u> at imaginary nails
In non-existent walls.

	Verb	Infinitive
1	'paddle'	to paddle
2	'strutting'	to strut
3	'clasped'	to clasp
4	'stump'	to stump
5	'tap'	to tap

VERBS: TASK 6D

From the verbs used in verse/stanza 1, I have the impression that the pigeons are

very active and busy. The different types of verbs – 'paddle', 'strutting', 'clasped', 'stump' and 'tap' – suggest the pigeons move in purposeful, self-important ways and the single syllables of 'stump' and 'tap' imply short, staccato movements.

VERBS: TASK 7

She <u>was</u> eaten by sharks.
She <u>has</u> swum around the rocks.
She <u>has/will have</u> been on holiday.

VERBS: TASK 8A

For this task you might write something like:

The poem is about a child stuck on top of a greenhouse, out of reach of the people below.

VERBS: TASK 8B

For this task you might write something like:

The title acts as a summary of what the poem is about and, straightaway, implies that it is dangerous as the word 'child' conveys a certain sense of defencelessness and vulnerability. A greenhouse – a structure made of glass – could easily break beneath the child, causing injury. That the child is 'on top of a greenhouse' suggests the possibility that he/she could fall from a height. The title makes me feel tense and anxious.

VERBS: TASK 8C

> *The wind billowing out the seat of my britches,*
> *My feet crackling splinters of glass and dried putty,*
> *The half-grown chrysanthemums staring up like accusers,*
> *Up through the streaked glass, flashing with sunlight,*
> *A few white clouds all rushing eastward,*
> *A line of elms plunging and tossing like horses,*
> *And everyone, everyone pointing up and shouting!*

You might write something like:

> *The nouns used suggest a rural setting as there is 'a line of elms'. The windy weather and rushing 'white clouds' combined with the 'splinters of glass' imply danger to the child's safety. The repetition of 'everyone' implies that the child is isolated.*

VERBS: TASK 8D

For this task you might write something like:

> *The speaker of the poem is the child, conveyed by the use of the first-person narrative. The child feels embarrassed to be the focus of everyone's angry attention. That 'everyone' is repeated stresses how uncomfortable the child feels to be singled out and how alone he or she feels up on the greenhouse with everyone else below, 'shouting'.*

Alternatively:

> *The speaker of the poem is the child, conveyed by the use of the first-person narrative. The child feels triumphant to be on top of the greenhouse with its wonderful views and is either delighted to be the centre of attention or annoyed that his/her enjoyment of the wind and views is being interrupted by the shouting people and the accusatory chrysanthemums.*

VERBS: TASK 8E

> *The wind billowing out the seat of my britches,*
> *My feet crackling splinters of glass and dried putty,*
> *The half-grown chrysanthemums staring up like accusers,*
> *Up through the streaked glass, flashing with sunlight,*
> *A few white clouds all rushing eastward,*
> *A line of elms plunging and tossing like horses,*
> *And everyone, everyone pointing up and shouting!*

VERBS: TASK 8F

The wind is billowing out the seat of my britches. My feet are crackling splinters of glass and dried putty. The half-grown chrysanthemums are staring up like accusers, up through the streaked glass, flashing with sunlight. A few white clouds are all rushing eastward. A line of elms is plunging and tossing like horses. And everyone, everyone is pointing up and shouting!

VERBS: TASK 9

She may have eaten contaminated food.

    (past participle = eaten; modal verbs = may, have)

They must have arrived by now.

    (past participle = arrived; modal verbs = must, have)

I shall be doing all I can to sort things out.

    (present participle = doing; modal verbs = shall, be)

She should not have spoken to me like that.

    (past participle = spoken; modal verbs = should, (not) have)

VERBS: TASK 10A

☐ Conformist   ☐ Angry   ☐ Miserable   ☑ Joyful   ☑ Defiant   ☑ Eccentric

VERBS: TASK 10B

For this task you might write something like:

The poem is called 'Warning' as the narrator wants to alert her audience to the fact that something unexpected and startling – possibly dangerous – is going to happen. As all that is going to happen is that, as an old person, she intends to be unconventional, the title is ironic but it serves its purpose: it catches our attention and is humorous for being an exaggeration.

VERBS: TASK 10C

When I am an old woman I <u>shall</u> wear purple

With a red hat which doesn't go, and doesn't suit me.

And I <u>shall</u> spend my pension on brandy and summer gloves

And satin sandals, and say we've no money for butter.

I <u>shall</u> sit down on the pavement when I'm tired

And gobble up samples in shops and press alarm bells

And run my stick along the public railings

And make up for the sobriety of my youth.

I <u>shall</u> go out in my slippers in the rain

And pick flowers in other people's gardens

And learn to spit.

You <u>can</u> wear terrible shirts and grow more fat

And eat three pounds of sausages at a go

Or only bread and pickle for a week

And hoard pens and pencils and beermats and things in boxes.

But now we <u>must</u> have clothes that keep us dry

And pay our rent and not swear in the street

And set a good example for the children.

We <u>must</u> have friends to dinner and read the papers.

But maybe I <u>ought</u> to practise a little now?

So people who know me are not too shocked and surprised

When suddenly I am old, and start to wear purple.

- I might do the high jump – <u>*uncertain*</u>

- I can do the high jump – <u>*certain*</u>

- I shall do the high jump – <u>*emphatic*</u>

VERBS: TASK 10D

Point (impression of the speaker)	Example(s)	Explanation	Marks 6
Defiant	'I shall wear purple'; 'I shall spend my pension'; 'I shall sit down'; 'I shall go out in my slippers'	The use of modal verbs suggests an emphatic and defiant tone	2
Extravagant	'brandy'; 'summer gloves'; 'satin sandals'	The choice of nouns suggests an unexpected delight in extravagant luxuries	2
Humorous and unruly	'gobble up'; 'spit'; 'hoard'	The choice of verbs suggests the actions of an unruly youth rather than an elderly lady	2

VERBS: TASK 11

The potential outcomes of this task are so broad that I have not included a suggested response.

VERBS: TASK 12

Verbs (infinitives)	Adjectives	Nouns
to lose	losing	loss
to know	knowing/knowledgeable	knowledge
to help	helpful/helping	help
to predict	predictable	prediction
to abandon	abandoned	abandonment
to be wise	wise	wisdom
to run	runny/running	run
to recur	recurring	recurrence

VERBS: TASK 13

The rustling leaves <u>were</u> <u>shimmering</u> in the evening breeze and, <u>having</u> <u>recovered</u> from <u>being</u> in the losing team, Maya's rate of breathing <u>eased</u>.

VERBS: TASK 14

Again, the potential outcomes of this task are so broad that I have not included a suggested response.

4. ADVERBS

Word	Word class	Meaning
tentatively	adverb	hesitantly
collaboratively	adverb	working together (like a team)
categorically	adverb	explicitly/directly/without question
gingerly	adverb	carefully/cautiously
surreptitiously	adverb	avoiding notice or attention/secretively
to deploy	verb	to use or to move into position
regional	adjective	relating to a region or district

ADVERBS: TASK 1

Tens of thousands of slightly damaged goods are being <u>unnecessarily</u> destroyed due to a defective screening system deployed at regional airports. Shipping agents <u>collaboratively</u> drafted an official statement to the Prime Minister in which their concerns were <u>categorically</u> stated. The Prime Minister has <u>informally</u> promised to address their issues <u>soon</u>.

You may have wanted to underline 'slightly', but that is an adjectival phrase describing the noun that follows it (goods), whereas 'unnecessarily', 'collaboratively', 'categorically', 'informally' and 'soon' all describe verbs.

ADVERBS: TASK 2

I used the adverbs to write this paragraph:

Yesterday morning, she tiptoed downstairs surreptitiously. She opened the kitchen cupboard and, gingerly, teased open the wrapping around the half-eaten chocolate cake. She was helplessly drawn to eating another slice when no one was looking. She knew that, soon, her mother would return and, suddenly, she heard footsteps approaching the back door. 'Hi, Mum!' she called, sleepily, and added, unnecessarily, 'Someone's been nibbling the cake again.'

5. PRONOUNS

Word	Word class	Meaning
to urge	verb	to encourage/to persuade gently
offspring	noun	children/progeny
boundary	noun	a line that marks the edge of an area
wicket	noun	the structure behind the batsman in a game of cricket
innings	noun	one of the divisions/moments of transition in a cricket match
to applaud	verb	to clap (demonstrating positive appreciation)
cholera	noun	an infectious disease

PRONOUNS: TASK 1

My boyfriend and I are thinking of getting married.

Sarah, Jane, Matthew and I will all be there.

It's time you and I had a chat.

She gave it to Gloria and me.

PRONOUNS: TASK 2A

Mr Michaels has a cat. Mr Michaels feeds his cat with meaty morsels. Mr Michaels knows that his cat loves meaty morsels.

PRONOUNS: TASK 2B

Mr Michaels has a cat. He feeds it meaty morsels. He knows that it loves them.

PRONOUNS: TASK 3

For this task you might write something like:

Mrs Briggs is irritated because Mr Briggs' use of the possessive adjective 'my' and the possessive pronoun 'his' when describing their son fails to acknowledge the role of Peter's mother, Mrs Briggs, although she is standing alongside Mr Briggs.

PRONOUNS: TASK 4A

For this task you might write something like:

The poem tells us that the son is resentful of his father for having been a distant parent and for not having been involved or interested in his life.

PRONOUNS: TASK 4B

For this task you might write something like:

> The speaker conveys his dissatisfaction with his father by the frequent use of 'you', which has the effect of creating an accusatory tone. Whenever he refers to the other fathers, by contrast, he uses pluralisation to suggest that his father is making his son feel different from the other boys, as they have fathers who join in and are light-hearted, 'joke with the masters' and are relaxed and 'at ease outside the pavilion'. The rhythm of the mantra 'Just passing. Spotted me through the railings' doesn't flow and sounds staccato, suggesting the awkwardness of the father's habitual behaviour around his son.

PRONOUNS: TASK 4C

For this task you might write something like:

> The title of the poem is appropriate as 'railings' suggests there is a physical barrier between the boy and his father at the school cricket match. There is also a metaphorical barrier between father and son which has been present at all the key moments in the boy's life. Railings can be seen through – unlike a wall or hedge – and this helps us to realise that the boy thinks he has seen through his father's excuses for being distant and remote, while feeling – very strongly – the obstacle between them. Railings are made of hard material and act as a firm, uncrossable barrier. The tone of the poem is sad. We only see things from the son's point of view and reasons for the father's distance may be complex and beyond the boy's understanding.

PRONOUNS: TASK 4D

You came to watch me playing cricket once.
Quite a few of the fathers did.
At ease, outside the pavilion
They would while away a Sunday afternoon.
Joke with the masters, urge on
their flannelled offspring. But not you.

Fielding deep near the boundary
I saw you through the railings.
You were embarrassed when I waved
and moved out of sight down the road.
When it was my turn to bowl though
I knew you'd still be watching.

Third ball, a wicket, and three more followed.
When we came in at the end of the innings
the other dads applauded and joined us for tea.
Of course, you had gone by then. Later,
you said you'd found yourself there by accident.
Just passing. Spotted me through the railings.

Speech-days • Prize-givings • School-plays
The Twentyfirst • The Wedding • The Christening
You would find yourself there by accident.
Just passing. Spotted me through the railings.

McGough uses the pronoun 'you' **nine times**.

PRONOUNS: TASK 4E

For this task you might write something like:

> *The effect of having someone single you out is to make you feel self-conscious, especially if they are part of a group and you are on your own.*

PRONOUNS: TASK 4F

For this task you might write something like:

> *They would feel uneasy because they would see one person being singled out as the focus of sustained attention from a group, which is a recognised feature of bullying.*

PRONOUNS: TASK 4G

The potential outcomes of this task are so broad that I have not included a suggested response.

PRONOUNS: TASK 5A

Yemen Crisis Appeal

Children in Yemen are struggling to survive bombs, terror and hunger. And right now <u>they're</u> dying from cholera. The disease is spreading fast. This deadly outbreak has already infected almost 400,000 children and adults.

A donation from <u>you</u> could help <u>us</u> save children's lives. Text ACT to 70008 to give £5. £40 of <u>your</u> money will buy a hygiene kit to protect children from this preventable disease.

PRONOUNS: TASK 5B

For this task you might write something like:

> *The use of the different pronouns is persuasive for different reasons. The second-person pronouns, 'you' and 'your', have the effect of making the reader feel directly addressed and therefore engaged. The use of the first-person plural pronoun, 'us' in this case but often 'we', has the effect of making the reader feel included or part of a group.*

PRONOUNS: TASK 5C

Pronoun	Effect
You ('A donation from you')	The use of the third-person plural pronoun makes it seem as if the number of children who need help is large.
They ('…they're dying…')	The use of the first-person plural pronoun makes the reader feel that by donating, she/he will be part of a team.
Us ('…could help us…')	The use of the second-person pronoun makes the reader feel personally addressed.

PRONOUNS: TASK 6A

a) the imperative:

> *'Text ACT to 70008'*

b) the future:

> *'£40 of your money will buy a hygiene kit…'*

PRONOUNS: TASK 6B

The imperative tense has the effect of being persuasive because

> *it injects a sense of urgency.*

The future tense has the effect of being persuasive because

> *it makes the reader envisage a better future situation with his/her help.*

6. PREPOSITIONS

Word	Word class	Meaning
cabinet	*noun*	*a type of cupboard*
oblivious	*adjective*	*unaware/unconcerned*
to throttle	*verb*	*to choke or strangle*

PREPOSITIONS: TASK 1

Beneath her fingertips, the velvet sofa was soft. Subconsciously, she explored its covered studs and played with a loose thread dangling from the padded arm, but Taiya's attention was not focused on the sofa's pink material or on anything else in that well-known room: not the leather-backed books in the glass cabinet above the desk nor the black and white family photographs arranged along the shelves. She was oblivious, too, to the sounds of tennis and games of 'it' rising from the school grounds beneath the window.

Her head was drawn back, its angle titled stiffly toward the suited man in front of her, towering above her and shouting angry words. Showers of spit sprang from the angry, writhing mouth. His eyes bulged as if he were being throttled by unseen hands. Taiya seemed to be taking it all in but she felt curiously detached, as though she were an invisible observer. The words seemed to bounce around her and glance off her school uniform as though it were some sort of bulletproof vest. Taiya stifled a sudden and totally inappropriate urge to laugh.

PREPOSITIONS: TASK 2

I used the prepositions **against, inside, on, behind** and **above** to write the following paragraph:

Against the orange walls and psychedelic cushions, the blue chairs seemed restful. Jana liked being inside. She sat down on one of the chairs and tried not to think about what was behind the drawn curtains. She glanced at the clock above the mantelpiece.

7. CONJUNCTIONS

Word	Word class	Meaning
abundance	noun	a large quantity
sparse	adjective	in short supply
elongating	verb	to make something longer

CONJUNCTIONS: TASK 1A

For this task you might respond:

The effect of a list connected with a series of 'ands' can be to suggest abundance.

CONJUNCTIONS: TASK 1B

Jenny Joseph uses the conjunction 'and' **24 times**.

CONJUNCTIONS: TASK 1C

For this task you might write something like:

The effect of this is to emphasise the number of different things she plans to do in old age and her enthusiasm for being so startling. It also adds a mischievous, child-like quality.

CONJUNCTIONS: TASK 2

The conjunction 'but' is used for the first time on line 16. The focus of time shifts from future to present.

8. WRITING STRUCTURES

Word	Word class	Meaning
component	noun	a part of a larger whole
cellar	noun	a room below ground level (for storage)
Dalmatian	noun	a breed of dog with a spotted coat
irony	noun	a type of sarcasm
to herald	verb	to signal that something is about to happen
rhetorical (question)	adjective	prompting an effect rather than an answer
to invoke	verb	to call on/appeal to someone

WRITING STRUCTURES: TASK 1

I added the following phrases:

> Mary ate her supper **in the kitchen**.
>
> The Dalmatian bounded in**to the cobbled stable yard**.
>
> The beech trees **beside the park** are shedding their leaves.

WRITING STRUCTURES: TASK 2

I added the following subordinate clauses:

I didn't look up.

> Although I wanted to, I didn't look up.

We became great friends.

> Soon after going to university, we became great friends.

I was secretly proud.

> I was secretly proud whenever my name was called out.

I tore a page from his notebook.

> Because he was unkind about my mother, I tore a page from his notebook.

WRITING STRUCTURES: TASK 3

Tony swam up beside me.

> Sensing I was in trouble, Tony swam up beside me.

I was lost.

> Taking the wrong turning, I was lost.

We went fishing together.

> Discovering a shared interest, we went fishing together.

The car broke down.

> Leaving the motorway, the car broke down.

WRITING STRUCTURES: TASK 4

Martha is two months older than me (**who**).

> *Martha, who is my best friend at school, is two months older than me.*

The weather is slowly improving (**which**).

> *The weather, which has been relentlessly cold, is slowly improving.*

My sister has learnt to write her full name (**whose**).

> *My sister, whose name is Leah, has learnt to write her full name.*

A local doctor came to visit (**in whom**).

> *A local doctor, in whom we had great faith, came to visit.*

WRITING STRUCTURES: TASK 5

subordinate clause   *main clause*

When Meg went to the shops, she bought some eggs.

subordinate clause   *main clause*

Although Grandpa Joe is unable to walk, he can do pilates.

main clause   *subordinate clause*

She can't come to tea, if she comes to lunch.

WRITING STRUCTURES: TASK 6

> *When I am older, I will own my own business.*

> *Bampton's river overflowed because of the heavy rain (**no need for a comma**).*

> *Feeling undermined, Zach behaved very badly.*

> *The jogger, who was 50 years old, barged into a woman on Wandsworth Bridge.*

WRITING STRUCTURES: TASK 7

	Phrase	Simple	Compound	Complex
Carrying fishing nets and jam jars on a string, my brothers came to collect me.				✓
Everyone was excited by the news.		✓		
Beyond any doubt	✓			
My mother talked of getting a new car when my father went back to work.				✓
He held my arm and steered me towards the towpath.			✓	
I was left alone in the garden.		✓		
A few days later	✓			
Mother, hearing the crash, ran up the stairs.				✓
I wrote a note to Jenny, which I got one of my brothers to deliver, that very night.				✓

9. CAPITAL LETTERS

Word	Word class	Meaning
twit	noun	a foolish person

CAPITAL LETTERS: TASK 1

I have a dog called 'Dog'. He was named by my sister, Sasha, when she was a toddler. A friend of ours called their dog 'Someone' because they couldn't agree on a name. In the park they were heard shouting, 'Someone, Someone! Come here at once.' Caroline Smith named her horse 'Like a Twit' so that as she entered the ring at the horse show the loudspeaker would announce, 'Here is Caroline Smith riding Like a Twit.'

10. FULL STOPS, EXCLAMATION MARKS AND QUESTION MARKS

Word	Word class	Meaning
squire	noun	a man of high social standing
inn	noun	a type of pub
rigging	noun	the system of ropes on sailing ships
gushing	adjective	effusive or exaggeratedly enthusiastic

FULL STOPS, EXCLAMATION MARKS AND QUESTION MARKS: TASK 1

The squire was staying at an inn by the docks. As we walked over there, I saw the port's long quays and a great fleet of ships at anchor. They were of all sizes and nations. The sailors in one ship were singing on the decks. In another, they were high in the rigging, hanging to threads that seemed no thicker than a spider's web.

FULL STOPS, EXCLAMATION MARKS AND QUESTION MARKS: TASK 2

Phrases:

'at an inn by the docks'; 'over there'; 'long quays'; 'a great fleet of ships at anchor'; 'all sizes and nations'; 'the sailors in one ship'; 'on the decks'; 'high in the rigging'; 'threads that seemed no thicker than a spider's web'.

Subordinate clauses:

'As we walked over there'; 'hanging to threads that seemed no thicker than a spider's web'.

Main clauses:

'The squire was staying at an inn by the docks.' 'They were of all sizes and nations.' 'The sailors in one ship were singing on the decks.'

A subordinate clause introduced with the relative pronoun 'that':

'that seemed no thicker than a spider's web'.

Present participle accompanied by an auxiliary verb:

'was staying'; 'were singing'.

A present participle introducing a subordinate clause (therefore without an auxiliary verb):

'hanging to threads that seemed no thicker than a spider's web'.

A subordinating conjunction:

'hanging to threads that seemed no thicker than a spider's web'.

A complex sentence:

'As we walked over there, I saw the port's long quays and a great fleet of ships at anchor.'

A compound sentence within a complex sentence:

'I saw the port's long quays and [I saw] a great fleet of ships at anchor.'

11. COMMAS, BRACKETS, DASHES AND HYPHENS

Word	Word class	Meaning
German shepherd	noun	a breed of dog, also known as an Alsatian

12. INDIRECT AND DIRECT SPEECH

Word	Word class	Meaning
bated (breath)	adjective	in great suspense
eruption	noun	a sudden outbreak of something

INDIRECT AND DIRECT SPEECH: TASK 1

This is how I used the lines of speech:

Tracey Green sipped her coffee. Her husband, Tony, was sitting opposite her, his face lit up by his iPad screen. He was engrossed in the morning's news.

April sun streamed through the kitchen window. It flared on the debris of breakfast mess: plates smeared with egg yolk, crumbs on the table and a nearly empty coffee pot. Tracey looked out at her garden and the brave group of shivering daffodils huddled conspiratorially beneath the apple tree.

She attempted conversation.

'I'm in Belfast next week.'

Tracey didn't expect an answer. She assumed that, as usual, Tony would be too engrossed. But, suddenly, she felt tension in the room.

'Keep your voice down,' *he hissed.* **'They're here.'**

Tony's face was frozen. His head was cocked on one side like a blackbird, mid-worm, that has suddenly detected danger.

Tracey felt the whizz of something tearing through the air and sensed its shadow on the kitchen wall.

'Watch out!' *she yelled. A brick smashed through the window, shattering the humdrum normality of the Greens' morning routine. It brought with it splinters of vicious broken glass and the sudden blast of cold air.*

They knew what to do. They had rehearsed for this moment so many times. Tony looked at Tracey and said, gravely, **'It's time.'**

13. APOSTROPHES

Word	Word class	Meaning
to omit	verb	to leave out
to possess	verb	to own
context	noun	understood within the 'setting' of other events

APOSTROPHES: TASK 1

Statement	Phrase
Robyn possesses a dog	Robyn's dog
The geese possess feathers	The geese's feathers
The child possesses a shoe	The child's shoe
The children possess a classroom	The children's classroom
The mouse possesses some cheese	The mouse's cheese
The girls possess some basketballs	The girls' basketballs

APOSTROPHES: TASK 2

Whos the partys candidate for vice president this year?

Who's the party's candidate for vice president this year?

The horses right foreleg was caught by the fences wire.

The horse's right foreleg was caught by the fence's wire.

Our neighbours car -a Nissan – has a scratch on its bonnet.

Our neighbour's car – a Nissan – has a scratch on its bonnet.

She did not hear her childrens cries.

She did not hear her children's cries.

The dogs bark was worse than its bite.

The dog's bark was worse than its bite.

The animals food was given to them every evening at 6.

The animals' food was given to them every evening at 6.

14. COLONS AND SEMICOLONS

Word	Word class	Meaning
provocative	adjective	deliberately causing an angry reaction
benevolence	noun	kindness
conspicuous	adjective	clearly visible
gratis	adverb	free/freely
filberts	noun	edible oval-shaped nuts
to entreat	verb	to ask someone anxiously to do something
to beseech	verb	to ask someone urgently to do something

COLONS AND SEMICOLONS: TASK 1

This is how the passage appears in *A Christmas Carol*:

> There were pears and apples, clustered high in blooming pyramids; there were bunches
> of grapes, made, in the shopkeepers' benevolence, to dangle from conspicuous hooks,
> that people's mouths might water gratis as they passed; there were piles of filberts,
> mossy and brown, recalling, in their fragrance, ancient walks among the woods, and
> pleasant shufflings ankle deep through withered leaves; there were Norfolk Biffins,
> squab and swarthy, setting off the yellow of the oranges and lemons, and, in the great
> compactness of their juicy persons, urgently entreating and beseeching to be carried
> home in paper bags and eaten after dinner.

COLONS AND SEMICOLONS: TASK 2

For this task you might write something like:

> Dickens creates a sense of abundance in various ways. First, he uses phrases to describe
> all the things seen, which increases their number. He also uses lists, extended with
> commas and semicolons, to detail everything seen and to increase the sense of plenty
> and abundance. His diction also implies plenty, such as 'clustered', 'piles' and 'great
> compactness'.

COLONS AND SEMICOLONS: TASK 3

This is how the passage appears in *North and South*:

> They did not speak; their hearts were too full. Another moment, and the train would be
> here; a minute more, and he would be gone.

It is, of course, perfectly possible to write these sentences without the commas that appear before 'and'.

15. FURTHER IDEAS FOR CREATIVITY, CRAFTSMANSHIP AND ANALYSIS

Word	Word class	Meaning
chronology	noun	arrangement of events/dates in order of occurrence
subtle	adjective	delicate and understated
subtleties	noun	quality or state of being subtle
to dispel	verb	to make disappear
derogatory	adjective	critical/disrespectful
pejorative	adjective	expressing contempt or disapproval
to depict	verb	to represent by drawing/painting/use of words
deterioration	noun	process of becoming progressively worse
to evoke	verb	to call to mind
capacity	noun	ability or power to do something
connotation	noun	underlying meaning/undertone
dilapidation	noun	process of falling into disrepair
emaciated	adjective	abnormally thin/weak
to juxtapose	verb	to place alongside for contrasting effect
adjacent	adjective	next to/alongside
to replicate	verb	to repeat/copy accurately
predatory	adjective	preying on others
introspection	noun	turned inwards
irresistible	adjective	unable to be resisted
to endorse	verb	to support or sanction
detrimental	adjective	harmful
covetous	adjective	wanting something for oneself
intriguing	adjective	interesting/captivating
to elicit	verb	to draw out
habitually	adverb	by way of habit
to advocate	verb	to recommend or support
indigenous	noun	originating or occurring naturally in a particular place

INDEX